"Much contemporary theology has turned to cultural studies as the partner of choice in its search for apt resources, drifting away from its unavoidable relationship with philosophy. In these circumstances it is a great pleasure to welcome a volume that charts a whole new phase in the mining of philosophy for the articulation and enrichment of robust forms of Christian theology. McCall has exactly the right kind of skills to execute this assignment: sure-footed theological grounding in the Christian tradition, well-honed appropriation of the philosophical sources, wonderful economy and clarity in exposition, and a discriminating voice of his own. This is a splendid introduction to an exciting new phase of Christian theology."
William J. Abraham, Perkins School of Theology, Southern Methodist University

"This timely and engaging book, written by one of today's leading practitioners of analytic theology, is a must-read for anyone interested in a careful, clear and accessible introduction to that burgeoning field."
Michael Rea, professor of philosophy, University of Notre Dame

"Analytic theology has quickly established itself as an important, dynamic research program in contemporary theology. But until now it has had no introductory text. Not only has Thomas McCall provided a stellar volume for just this purpose; he also makes a contribution to the theological literature by showing that analytic theology is not merely philosophical theology masquerading as systematic theology—it is a truly *theological* theology. This is a clear, well-written and compelling work that is sure to be of great interest to a wide readership."
Oliver Crisp, professor of systematic theology, Fuller Theological Seminary

"At the outset of this extraordinary and much-needed book, Tom McCall promises to introduce nonspecialists to analytic theology. He superbly accomplishes this task, but so much more. No mere introduction, this book engages constructively with a wide variety of theologians and philosophers on central theological topics. McCall's balance and lucidity make this a breakthrough book, not only for the project of analytic theology, but also for the full arrival of McCall's charitable and wise theological voice."
Matthew Levering, Perry Family Foundation Professor of Theology, Mundelein Seminary

"With a lively combination of theoretical and constructive work, Tom McCall not only introduces but contributes to the budding discipline of analytic theology. Deftly moving between clarifications and programmatic statements on the one hand and case studies on the other, McCall has written a book that will interest student and scholar alike."
Kevin Hector, assistant professor of theology and the philosophy of religions, The University of Chicago Divinity School

An Invitation to

ANALYTIC CHRISTIAN THEOLOGY

Thomas H. McCall

IVP Academic
An imprint of InterVarsity Press
Downers Grove, Illinois

InterVarsity Press
P.O. Box 1400, Downers Grove, IL 60515-1426
ivpress.com
email@ivpress.com

InterVarsity Press® is the book-publishing division of InterVarsity Christian Fellowship/USA®, a movement of students and faculty active on campus at hundreds of universities, colleges and schools of nursing in the United States of America, and a member movement of the International Fellowship of Evangelical Students. For information about local and regional activities, visit intervarsity.org.

All Scripture quotations, unless otherwise indicated, are taken from THE HOLY BIBLE, NEW INTERNATIONAL VERSION®, NIV® Copyright © 1973, 1978, 1984, 2011 by Biblica, Inc.™ Used by permission. All rights reserved worldwide.

Cover design: David Fassett
Interior design: Beth McGill

Images: Geometric abstract: © marigold_88/iStockphoto
Celtic knotwork: © imacon/iStockphoto

ISBN 978-0-8308-4095-3 (print)
ISBN 978-0-8308-9930-2 (digital)

Printed in the United States of America ∞

Library of Congress Cataloging-in-Publication Data
McCall, Thomas H.
  An invitation to analytic Christian theology / Thomas H. McCall.
    pages cm
  Includes bibliographical references and index.
  ISBN 978-0-8308-4095-3 (pbk. : alk. paper)
  1. Theology—Methodology. 2. Analysis (Philosophy) 3. Philosophical theology. I. Title.
  BR118.M24 2015
  230'.046—dc23

                                                                    2015033451

P 23 22 21 20 19 18 17 16 15 14 13 12 11 10 9 8 7 6 5 4 3 2 1

Y 35 34 33 32 31 30 29 28 27 26 25 24 23 22 21 20 19 18 17 16 15

To Bill Ury, my first and finest teacher of theology.

You showed me what it means to do theology to the glory of God and

for the sake of the world, and you helped me catch a precious glimpse

of "love divine, all loves excelling." I'll be forever grateful.

Contents

Contents

Introduction

THE WIDE RANGE OF EVENTS and publications that are loosely gathered under the label "analytic theology" is both quite broad and very active. Proponents and practitioners range from traditionally minded Orthodox and Roman Catholic philosophers and theologians through Anglican, Lutheran, Methodist and other tradition-sensitive scholars to conservative evangelicals and to revisionist or "progressive" theologians. In some quarters, enthusiasm runs high. In other sectors of the theological (and philosophical) academy, suspicion and even hostility run deep. Misunderstanding often accompanies the label, and questions abound. But just what is this thing called "analytic theology"? What are its "accidental" features, and what are its "essential" attributes? And what are we to make of it *as theology*? Or is it merely a technically precise and agenda-driven subdiscipline of analytic metaphysics? Where is it going? Is there some discernible direction that it will—or should—take?

In this book, I introduce nonspecialists to analytic theology. I try to make clear both what it *isn't* and what it *is*. Accordingly, I discuss what makes analytic theology *analytic*, and I try to lay out what makes analytic theology really *theology*. Specifically, I outline analytic theology's connections to Scripture, Christian tradition and culture (broadly conceived), and I do so by using case studies to illuminate the relationships and the need for further integration. Here I must also confess to an agenda: I am hoping to influence the future of analytic theology by calling the discipline to a deeper engagement with the traditional resources of the theological task.

I come to the work of analytic theology as someone who is, by training and by vocation, a theologian. Thus I am especially grateful for the patience and graciousness of those friends and colleagues who have genuine expertise in epistemology, metaphysics and philosophy of religion (as well as the history of philosophy). I am deeply indebted to you for whatever abilities I have as an analytic theologian, and I am truly grateful for your collegiality and encouragement. I am also thankful for those fellow theologians who have taken up the mantle of analytic theology; and I am grateful as well to those who led the way by actually doing it before it was ever called by that name. Oliver Crisp, Mike Rea and Billy Abraham read the manuscript and offered very helpful critique and encouragement, and the book is much improved as a result. (All remaining faults are, of course, entirely mine.)

In addition, I am grateful for the community of saints and scholars who surround me at Trinity Evangelical Divinity School (and especially the members of the Deerfield Dialogue Group who read part of the manuscript), and I am indebted as well to the administration and the board of regents for a sabbatical in the fall of 2014.

1

What Is Analytic Theology?

Fear of scholasticism is the mark of the false prophet.

KARL BARTH

A BRIEF HISTORY OF ANALYTIC THEOLOGY

Where we were: The revival of philosophy of religion. For a good deal of the twentieth century, academic philosophy—especially Anglo-American "analytic" philosophy—was often taken to be hostile to traditional theistic belief in general and perhaps especially so to Christian belief.[1] Logical positivism insisted that theological claims were not only false but indeed meaningless, and many philosophers found it difficult even to take theology seriously. The conclusions of A. J. Ayer are both representative and influential. He claims that the very "possibility of religious knowledge" has been "ruled out by our treatment of metaphysics."[2] If the "criterion of verifiability" eliminates metaphysics, and if theology is only a subcategory of metaphysics, then theology is obviously eliminated—the very *possibility* has been ruled out and all God-talk is literally

Epigraph: Karl Barth, *Church Dogmatics*, vol. I/1, *The Doctrine of the Word of God*, ed. T. F. Torrance, trans. Geoffrey Bromiley (Edinburgh: T & T Clark, 1975), p. 279.
[1]I realize that (at least on some understandings of the term) the story of analytic theology far predates the modern era and indeed has far more in common with scholasticism than it does with either twentieth-century philosophy or modern theology. More on this anon.
[2]Alfred Jules Ayer, *Language, Truth, and Logic* (New York: Dover, 1952), p. 114.

nonsensical.[3] Hud Hudson says, "Informed that questions about the existence, nature, and significance of the deity were hereafter to be engaged exclusively under the guidance of linguistic analyses of religious language, and menaced with (inexplicably popular) verificationist theories of meaning, theologians were told by analytic philosophers that they had not even achieved the minimal distinction of saying anything false, for they had not managed to say anything at all."[4]

The response of many theologians in the late modern era to the developments in mainstream philosophy in Anglo-American circles was understandable: they largely ignored the work of these philosophers and looked elsewhere for intellectual resources and conversation partners. Some sought refuge in "Continental" philosophy, while others decried any engagement between philosophy and theology.

But the second half of the twentieth century witnessed some remarkable changes. As Hudson notes, "This most unfortunate moment in the history of analytic philosophy was mercifully temporary, as was its slavish devotion to linguistic analyses, verificationism, and all the unfounded suspicion of metaphysics, ethics, and religion that followed in its wake."[5] Logical positivism couldn't bear its own weight, and Ayer's confident pronouncements are now valued more as a quaint museum artifact of philosophical history ("Look, kids, isn't it amazing that anyone ever said that—and especially that he seemed so cocksure about it?") than as a helpful repository of philosophical insight. With the collapse of positivism came a rebirth of serious metaphysics—and with that collapse and the rebirth of metaphysics came a revival of philosophy of religion.[6] Where philosophical consideration of theological issues had been deemed an utter waste of time, now it was seen as an interesting area of inquiry. Serious and sustained engagement with perennial issues of religious and theological interest was happening again, and many of the philosophers

---

[3]Ibid., p. 35.
[4]Hud Hudson, *The Fall and Hypertime* (Oxford: Oxford University Press, 2014), p. 4.
[5]Ibid., p. 5.
[6]For a telling of this tale, see Nicholas Wolterstorff, "How Philosophical Theology Became Possible Within the Analytic Tradition of Philosophy," in *Analytic Theology: New Essays in the Philosophy of Theology*, ed. Oliver D. Crisp and Michael C. Rea (Oxford: Oxford University Press, 2009), pp. 155-68.

engaged in this work were—and are—committed Christians.

Not all philosophers rejoice at these developments, but it is increasingly hard for them not to notice them. Quentin Smith describes—and decries—this development:

> The secularization of mainstream academia began to quickly unravel upon the publication of Plantinga's influential book on realist theism, *God and Other Minds*, in 1967. It became apparent to the philosophical profession that this book displayed that realist theists were not outmatched by naturalists in terms of the most valued standards of academic philosophy: conceptual precision, rigor of argumentation, technical erudition, and an in-depth defense of an original worldview. This book, followed seven years later by Plantinga's even more impressive book, *The Nature of Necessity*, made it manifest that a realist theist was writing at the highest qualitative level of analytic philosophy, on the same playing field as Carnap, Russell, Grünbaum, and other naturalists.[7]

Smith, in what basically amounts to something of an alarmist "call to arms" to his fellow atheists, concludes that "God is not 'dead' in academia; he returned to life in the late 1960's and is now alive and well in his last academic stronghold, philosophy departments."[8]

While triumphalism on the part of Christian philosophers would be both very premature and unseemly (they remain, by all measures, in the substantial minority within academic philosophy), nonetheless Smith is right that the situation is very different than it was only a few decades ago. The Society of Christian Philosophers, founded in 1978 as a small group of diverse scholars who were more unified by common interests than by shared commitment to a particular creed, now has in the neighborhood of a thousand members. Several journals—notably *Faith and Philosophy, Philosophia Christi, Religious Studies, Sophia, Philo* and the *International Journal of Philosophy of Religion*—are devoted to issues broadly related to the study of the philosophy of religion, and Christian philosophers are very active in these and other venues. At the same time, Christian philosophers are very active in other, more "mainstream" areas of contemporary philosophy; important, recent work in metaphysics and

---

[7]Quentin Smith, "The Metaphilosophy of Naturalism," *Philo* 4, no. 2 (2001): 2.
[8]Ibid., p. 3.

epistemology in particular has been influenced by philosophers with religious interests and well-known Christian commitments.

Not surprisingly, the growth of Christian involvement in philosophy has been accompanied by increased interest in issues of perennial concern in philosophy of religion. Work on such issues had never entirely disappeared, of course, for prominent philosophers such as Basil Mitchell, Peter Geach, Austin Farrer and others were making significant contributions well before the current renaissance of Christian philosophy really took off.[9] However, engagement has been growing at an astounding rate. Issues surrounding religious pluralism and exclusivism, problems of evil (including not only the "logical" problem of evil but also "evidential" problems), religious epistemology, religious experience, miracles, theistic arguments (particularly various versions of ontological, cosmological, teleological and moral arguments) and science and religion have been explored with impressive vigor and analyzed with formidable rigor.[10] Positions have been set out and explained, attacked and defended, modified and surrendered. The work in philosophy of religion has not been cordoned off from other, more "mainstream" philosophical work. To the contrary, in many ways it has remained vitally engaged with

---

[9]E.g., Basil Mitchell, *The Justification of Religious Belief* (Oxford: Oxford University Press, 1981); Mitchell, *Faith and Criticism* (Oxford: Oxford University Press, 1995); Mitchell, *Morality, Religious and Secular: The Dilemma of the Traditional Conscience* (Oxford: Oxford University Press, 1986); Peter Geach, *God and the Soul* (South Bend, IN: St. Augustine's Press, 1969); Geach, *Providence and Evil* (Cambridge: Cambridge University Press, 1977); Geach, *The Virtues* (Cambridge: Cambridge University Press, 1977); Geach, *Logic Matters* (Berkeley: University of California Press, 1972); Austin Farrer, *The Freedom of the Will* (London: Black, 1958); Farrer, *Love Almighty and Ills Unlimited: An Essay on Providence and Evil* (London: Collins, 1961); Farrer, *Saving Belief: A Study of Essentials* (London: Hodder & Stoughton, 1964); Farrer, *Faith and Speculation: An Essay in Philosophical Theology* (London: Black, 1967).

[10]The contents—and perhaps the very existence—of the numerous and massive "handbooks" and "companions" to philosophy of religion bear weighty testimony to this fact. See, e.g., William J. Wainwright, ed., *The Oxford Handbook of Philosophy of Religion* (New York: Oxford University Press, 2005); Philip L. Quinn and Charles Taliaferro, eds., *A Companion to Philosophy of Religion* (Oxford: Blackwell, 1997); William E. Mann, ed., *The Blackwell Guide to the Philosophy of Religion* (Oxford: Blackwell, 2005); Michael L. Peterson and Raymond J. VanArragon, eds., *Contemporary Debates in Philosophy of Religion* (Oxford: Blackwell, 2004); J. P. Moreland and William Lane Craig, eds., *The Blackwell Companion to Natural Theology* (Oxford: Blackwell, 2009); Justin McBrayer and Daniel Howard-Snyder, eds., *The Blackwell Companion to the Problem of Evil* (Oxford: Blackwell, 2013); Chad Meister and Paul Copan, eds., *The Routledge Companion to Philosophy of Religion*, 2nd ed. (New York: Routledge, 2013). See also the impressive series Oxford Studies in Philosophy of Religion, edited by Jon Kvanvig.

cutting-edge work in epistemology, ethics and metaphysics; to use the latter as an example, from Alvin Plantinga's early work *The Nature of Necessity* to Brian Leftow's recent contributions in *God and Necessity*, important work in the metaphysics of modality has been deeply—and some might say "essentially"—connected to philosophy of religion.[11] Judging from the interest and output, analytic philosophy of religion is not only alive and well but indeed healthy and robust.

How we got here: From philosophy of religion to philosophical theology. But for all the vigor and intellectual energy that is captured and reflected in work on general or generic issues in philosophy of religion, the interests of Christian philosophers have not been limited to those issues. Instead, Christian philosophers have been deeply interested in distinctly *Christian theological* topics, and they have devoted much energy to the analysis and defense of Christian doctrine. The past few decades have witnessed important work on the doctrine of revelation (and divine speech); the inspiration, authority and interpretation of the Christian Scriptures; divine attributes (particularly simplicity, necessity, aseity, omnipotence, omniscience, eternity and freedom); divine action in creation; providence; miraculous intervention; theological anthropology; original sin; incarnation; atonement; resurrection; and eschatology.[12]

Where we are: Philosophical theology and analytic theology. More recently, the term *analytic theology* has come into use. There are, of course, important forebears to this work: David Kelsey, Nicholas Wolterstorff and others at Yale; disparate figures such as William P. Alston, Norman Kretzmann, George Mavrodes, Keith Yandell and others elsewhere in the United States; Paul Helm and Richard Swinburne in the United Kingdom; and Vincent Brummer and others of the Utrecht

---

[11]See Alvin Plantinga, *The Nature of Necessity* (Oxford: Oxford University Press, 1974); and Brian Leftow, *God and Necessity* (Oxford: Oxford University Press, 2012). See also the recent proposals of Hugh J. McCann, *Creation and the Sovereignty of God* (Bloomington: Indiana University Press, 2012).

[12]Once again, the proliferation of "readers," "handbooks" and "companions" stands as evidence of the breadth and depth of the work undertaken; e.g., Oliver D. Crisp, ed., *A Reader in Contemporary Philosophical Theology* (New York: T & T Clark, 2009); Michael C. Rea, ed., *Oxford Readings in Philosophical Theology*, 2 vols. (Oxford: Oxford University Press, 2009); Thomas P. Flint and Michael C. Rea, eds., *The Oxford Handbook of Philosophical Theology* (Oxford: Oxford University Press, 2009); Charles Taliaferro and Chad Meister, eds., *The Cambridge Companion to Christian Philosophical Theology* (Cambridge: Cambridge University Press, 2010).

school of philosophical theology in the Netherlands. Following trail-
blazers such as these, and building on the recent renaissance of metaphysics and philosophy of religion, the analytic theology movement is
now growing. The publication of the volume *Analytic Theology: Essays
in the Philosophy of Theology*, edited by Oliver D. Crisp and Michael C.
Rea, marked an important moment. The Analytic Theology Project
(sponsored and promoted by Notre Dame's Center for Philosophy of
Religion as well the University of Innsbruck in Austria and the Shalem
Center in Jerusalem, and funded by generous grants from the John Tem-
pleton Foundation) with its annual Logos conference and other activities,
the launch of the *Journal of Analytic Theology*, and the inauguration of
the book series Oxford Studies in Analytic Theology all lend support to
this growing movement.

The meaning of the term *analytic theology* can vary in common par-
lance, and it is safe to say that there is no single, decisively settled meaning
of the term when it is used as a label. Still, perhaps we can safely say that
what is common across the range of uses is this: *analytic theology* sig-
nifies a commitment to employ the conceptual tools of analytic philosophy where those tools might be helpful in the work of constructive
Christian theology. Scholars will, naturally enough, disagree among
themselves about just which of those tools are most helpful, which
projects are best served by their use and other matters, but on the whole
such a minimalist characterization seems safe enough. William J.
Abraham offers this helpful summary: analytic theology "can be usefully
defined as follows: it is systematic theology attuned to the skills, resources, and virtues of analytic philosophy."[13] As such, analytic theology
is a growing and energetic field at the intersections of philosophy of religion and systematic theology.

WHAT ANALYTIC THEOLOGY *IS* (OR SHOULD BE)

Such minimalist characterization, while fairly safe, does not take us very
far. What, more precisely, is one doing when one does analytic theology?

---

[13]William J. Abraham, "Systematic Theology as Analytic Theology," in *Analytic Theology: New
Essays in the Philosophy of Theology*, ed. Oliver D. Crisp and Michael C. Rea (Oxford: Oxford
University Press, 2009), p. 54.

Just what *is* analytic theology? Perhaps it will help first to consider what is so *analytic* about analytic theology. Following this, we shall think about how it is an exercise in *theology*.

Analytic theology as analytic *theology*. As we have seen, Quentin Smith praises Plantinga's work for its excellence in "the most valued standards of analytic philosophy: conceptual precision, rigor of argumentation, technical erudition, and an in-depth defense of an original worldview."[14] Oliver D. Crisp echoes this estimation of what counts as good work in analytic philosophy; he observes that analytic philosophy is characterized by "a logical rigour, clarity, and parsimony of expression, coupled with attention to a certain cluster of philosophical problems."[15] Analytic theology is relevantly similar, he says, for it "will prize intellectual virtues like clarity, parsimony of expression, and argumentative rigour."[16] Michael C. Rea's description of analytic philosophy echoes these accounts in some ways. While recognizing that clear and sharp lines between "analytic" and "nonanalytic" (or "Continental") philosophical approaches are neither easy to come by nor perhaps really worth all the work, he characterizes analytic approaches to philosophy in terms of *style* and *ambition*.[17] The ambitions are generally "to identify the scope and limits of our powers to obtain knowledge of the world," and "to provide such true explanatory theories as we can in areas of inquiry (metaphysics, morals, and the like) that fall outside the scope of the natural sciences."[18] Rea characterizes the style as including the following prescriptions:

> P1. Write as if philosophical positions and conclusions can be adequately formulated in sentences that can be formalized and logically manipulated.

> P2. Prioritize precision, clarity, and logical coherence.

> P3. Avoid substantive (non-decorative) use of metaphor and other tropes whose semantic content outstrips their propositional content.

---

[14]Smith, "Metaphilosophy," p. 2.

[15]Oliver D. Crisp, "On Analytic Theology," in Crisp and Rea, *Analytic Theology*, p. 35.

[16]Ibid., pp. 37-38.

[17]Michael C. Rea, introduction to Crisp and Rea, *Analytic Theology*, pp. 3-4. See also Nick Trakakis, "Meta-Philosophy of Religion: The Analytic-Continental Divide in Philosophy of Religion," *Ars Disputandi* 7 (2007): 179-220.

[18]Rea, introduction, p. 4.

P4. Work as much as possible with well-understood primitive concepts, and concepts that can be analyzed in terms of those.

P5. Treat conceptual analysis (insofar as possible) as a source of evidence.[19]

This much, at least, is characteristic of analytic philosophy. So what about analytic theology? As Rea sees things, "analytic theology is just the activity of approaching theological topics with the ambitions of an analytic philosopher and in a style that conforms to the prescriptions that are distinctive of analytic philosophical discourse. It will also involve, more or less, pursuing those topics in a way that engages the literature that is constitutive of the analytic tradition, employing some of the technical jargon from that tradition, and so on. But in the end, it is the style and ambitions that are most central."[20]

All this is helpful, but perhaps a bit more explanation would be beneficial. Consider P1. This need not mean that all meaningful statements in theology (or philosophy) need to be expressed formally; it should not be taken to mean that every theological claim should be stated in an apparatus with numbered propositions and a formal structure. What it does mean, however, is that the default setting for theologians should be to communicate propositions that could be expressed this way. For as Rea says, "absent special circumstances," things have "gone very much amiss" if a view "is expressed in such a way that it has no clear logical outcomes."[21]

Consider also P2. This need not—and should not—be taken to mean that logical precision and coherence are the only important criteria for a theologian, and neither should it be taken to imply even that logical precision and coherence are the most important criteria. The theologian who is convinced that her first commitment is fidelity to the priority and ultimacy of divine revelation should have no difficulty in assenting to P2. Neither, further, should P2 be taken to imply that the same levels of logical precision are possible with all theological topics, nor yet that all theological projects require the same levels of precision and argumentative

---

[19]Ibid., pp. 5-6.
[20]Ibid., p. 7.
[21]Ibid., p. 5 n. 5.

rigor. Consider, by way of example, children's catechetical literature. Surely this literature is *theological*, but it neither can nor should attempt to display the same level of logical precision or argumentative rigor as, say, advanced work in scholastic theology. P2 does not clam that such theological literature should do so, or that all work in theology must always do so.

Neither should P2 be misunderstood with respect to claims about the importance of "clarity." Rea notes that this claim can seem ironic "in light of the fact that quite a lot of analytic philosophy [and, we could add, some analytic theology] is very difficult even for specialists, and totally inaccessible to non-specialists."[22] But "clear" does not mean "easy." Instead, it expresses a commitment to the work of "spelling out hidden assumptions, scrupulously trying to lay bare whatever evidence one has (or lacks) for the claims that one is making, and on taking care to confine one's vocabulary to ordinary language, well-understood primitive concepts, and technical jargon definable in terms of these."[23] Finally, we should note that P2 does not imply that everything (or everything worth talking about) in theology will become crystal clear. The goal of analytic theology is not (or at least need not be) the removal of all mystery in theology. To the contrary, analytic philosophers of religion have long been keenly aware of the place of mystery in theology, and it may be that at certain points an important role of the theologian is to clarify just where the mystery really lies. P2 does not suggest that analytic theology will make everything "clear" in the sense that it makes everything "easy and readily accessible to the nonspecialist." Instead, what it prioritizes is clarity to the appropriate audiences and to the greatest possible degree. And it insists that "mystery" must not be confused with logical incoherence, and it likewise insists that we do not glorify what is clearly incoherent with the shroud of "mystery." As Alan G. Padgett says, theology should "seek the truth about God" and "therefore must shun incoherence and irrationality."[24] Where "sometimes 'mystery' is evoked as an excuse

---

[22]Ibid., p. 5 n. 6.

[23]Ibid.

[24]Alan G. Padgett, "The Trinity in Theology and Philosophy: Why Jerusalem Should Work with Athens," in *Philosophical and Theological Essays on the Trinity*, ed. Thomas McCall and Michael C. Rea (Oxford: Oxford University Press, 2009), p. 332.

for sloppy thinking, this must be anathema to any academic theology worthy of the name." For "after all, the mystery of God does not end when theology speaks clearly. The simple phrase, 'Jesus loves me, this I know, for the Bible tells me so,' covers vast, deep mysteries that even the angels gaze into with awe and wonder."[25]

P3 rules out "substantive (non-decorative) use of metaphor and other tropes whose semantic content outstrips their propositional content." This does not, or at least need not, mean that there is no valid or valuable place for metaphor in theology. Analytic theologians will disagree among themselves as to how—and how much—metaphor is useful and legiti-mate.[26] But the basic point is fairly plain: on P3, theologians are not at liberty to trade loosely in metaphor without ever being able to specify just what is meant by those metaphors. They are not, then, free to make claims the meaning of which cannot be specified or spelled out. Theolo-gians are not licensed to trade in what Randal Rauser calls "unclarifiable unclarity."[27] P4 calls the analytic theologian to work with "well-understood primitive concepts" that are reasonably taken to be basic, intuitive or (minimally) uncontroversial (and with concepts that can be understood in terms of such primitive concepts). Some theologians will be quick to raise concerns here; they will worry that the very notion of "well-understood primitive concepts" may both conceal blind spots of social location and privilege and be a Procrustean bed that restricts theological concepts to "what we already know to be true" and thus curtails the possibility of engagement with divine revelation. But once again, it is important not to misunderstand P4. The "as much as possible" is key here; if the preunderstood concepts don't do enough work, then some of them can be adjusted. Others won't be so easy to adjust or discard, but this category of primitive concepts is both quite small and very basic (e.g., the law of noncontradiction). Simply put, there is no good reason to

---

[25]Ibid.

[26]I thank Billy Abraham for pressing this point. The "standard" work on metaphor in theology remains Janet Martin Soskice, *Metaphor and Religious Language* (Oxford: Oxford University Press, 1987).

[27]Randal Rauser, "Theology as a Bull Session," in Crisp and Rea, *Analytic Theology*, pp. 74-75. See also Harry Frankfurt, *On Bullshit* (Princeton, NJ: Princeton University Press, 2005); and Frank-furt, *Bullshit and Philosophy*, ed. Gary L. Hardcastle and George A. Resich (Chicago: Open Court, 2005).

think that the notion of "well-understood primitive concepts" *must* function as a Procrustean bed.

Finally, Rea says that P5 calls us to "treat conceptual analysis (insofar as it is possible) as a source of evidence." It should be obvious that he does not say that conceptual analysis is the *only* source of evidence, and there is no reason to think that it should be taken this way. Neither does he claim that conceptual analysis is the *primary* or *ultimate* source of evidence. P5 makes an important claim, but it is a rather modest one. What it insists on is this: if close conceptual analysis reveals that some theological proposition *P* is, say, internally inconsistent, then that analysis gives us all the evidence we need to reject *P.* No matter how grand the claims of *P*'s supporters in defense of the supporting evidence *for* it, if *P* is incoherent (self-referentially or otherwise), then it is not true. Once we have established that *P* is incoherent (which is a task much harder than is sometimes supposed), we have all the reason we need to conclude that it is wrong. In addition, of course, conceptual analysis might count as evidence in other and more positive ways as well. Consider perfect being theology, for example: here theologians analyze "perfection" and then take deliverances of that analysis as evidence in support of their theological conclusions.

Much more could be said about what makes analytic theology truly *analytic,* of course. While this could be expanded on and broadened (particularly in directions that put less of a premium on precision), Rea's P1-P5 give us an initial sense of what it means to say that theology is analytic theology. Generally speaking, analytic theology is theology that is attuned to and committed to the "goals and ambitions" of analytic philosophy: a commitment to truth wherever it may be found, clarity of expression, and rigor of argumentation. Very often it will not hesitate to make appropriate use of the available tools of analytic philosophy, especially as these aid conceptual precision and argumentative rigor.

***Analytic theology as analytic* theology.** But if, echoing Smith, it is the concern with "conceptual precision" and "rigor of argumentation" that makes analytic theology *analytic,* then what is it that makes analytic theology really *theology*? This book develops an answer to this question, but an initial summary may help. Recall that Smith talks not only about "conceptual precision" and "rigor of argumentation" but also about "technical erudition" and the "in-depth defense of an original worldview." For the analytic philosopher, "technical erudition" will naturally involve mastery of the requisite field (metaphysics, philosophy of mind, epistemology, etc.), but it may also include competence in other, related fields (biology for philosophy of biology, neurology for philosophy of mind, etc.). For the analytic theologian, such erudition will include competence in the relevant areas of philosophical study that are necessary for "conceptual precision" and "rigor of argumentation." But for the analytic theologian qua theologian, it must involve much more than this. For unless analytic theology is merely "armchair theology" (albeit armchair theology done by very bright people), it will be grounded in the Christian Scriptures, it will be informed by the great tradition of doctrinal development, it will be "christologically normed" and it will be culturally engaged. As theology, it will seek to articulate what we may know of God as God has revealed himself to us. As Nicholas Wolterstorff puts it to theologians:

> Do not be ersatz philosophers, do not be ersatz cultural theorists, do not be ersatz anything. Be genuine theologians. Be sure-footed in philosophy. . . . But then: be theologians. . . . What we need to hear from you is how things look when seen in light of the triune God—may his name be praised!—who creates and sustains us, who redeems us, and who will bring this frail and fallen, though yet glorious, humanity and cosmos to consummation.[28]

Accordingly, analytic theology is theology done by theologians who are "sure-footed" in philosophy (many of whom will have extensive training and professional expertise there, and indeed may be leaders within their field), but it is a kind of theology nonetheless.

Such a conception of theology is, of course, not remotely new. What we may usefully refer to as "analytic theology" is very similar in many respects to deeply traditional ways of doing theology. We can see this kind of work exemplified in the theology of the scholastics (both medieval and post-Reformation/early modern). So in some sense, the re-

---

[28]Nicholas Wolterstorff, "To Theologians: From One Who Cares About Theology but Is Not One of You," *Theological Education* (2005): 91-92.

birth of analytic theology may be thought of as scholasticism redivivus. As Richard Swinburne—surely a pioneer of analytic theology—says, "large-scale theology needs clear and rigorous argument," and it is "high time for theology to return" to the standards set by Thomas Aquinas, John Duns Scotus and others.[29] But it is not only the "high scholastics" who worked this way, for we can also witness many of these virtues in theologians from the patristics to the pietists.[30] Many theologians in the Christian tradition were concerned with both "conceptual precision" and "argumentative rigor" as well as "technical erudition" and the "in-depth defense of an original worldview."

Consider what John Wesley—an evangelist hardly known as a "scholastic" or an "analytic theologian"—has to say about the importance of acquiring the tools for "conceptual precision" and "argumentative rigor." Logic, he says, is "necessary next to, and in order to, the knowledge of Scripture."[31] Despite the fact that it is "now quite unfashionable," nonetheless logic is invaluable. For with it we have the possibility of "apprehending things clearly, judging truly, and reasoning conclusively."[32] And as with logic, so also with metaphysics. Thus Wesley will ask of clergy:

> Am I a tolerable master of the sciences? Have I gone through the very gate of them, logic? If not, I am not likely to go much further, when I stumble at the threshold. Do I understand it so as to be ever the better for it? To have it always ready for use; so as to apply every rule of it, when occasion is, almost as naturally as I turn my hand? Do I understand it at all? . . . Can I reduce an indirect mood to a direct, a hypothetic to a categorical syllogism? Rather, have not my stupid indolence and laziness made me very ready to believe, what the little wits and pretty gentlemen affirm, "that logic is good for nothing"? It is good for this at least (wherever it is understood), to make people talk less; by showing them both what is, and what is not, to the point; and how extremely

---

[29]Richard Swinburne, *The Coherence of Theism*, 2nd ed. (Oxford: Oxford University Press, 1993), p. 7.

[30]See, e.g., Gregory of Nyssa, *Against Eunomius* 1.42, *Nicene and Post-Nicene Fathers*, ed. Philip Schaff, series 2 (1886–1889; repr., Peabody, MA: Hendrickson, 1994), 5:98-99 (Patrologia Graeca [= *Patrologiae Cursus Completus*: Series Graeca], ed. Jacques-Paul Migne [Paris, 1857–1886], 45:460-61).

[31]John Wesley, "Address to the Clergy," in *The Works of John Wesley*, vol. 10, *Letters, Essays, Dialogs, and Addresses* (Grand Rapids: Zondervan, n.d.), p. 483.

[32]Ibid.

hard it is to prove anything. Do I understand metaphysics; if not the depths of the Schoolmen, the subtleties of Scotus or Aquinas, yet the first rudiments, the general principles, of that useful science?[33]

Consider further what Wesley says about the importance of "technical erudition" in theology. Insisting on the importance of knowledge of the scope of Christian Scripture as well as facility in the relevant ancient languages, he asks:

Have I, (1) such a knowledge of Scripture, as becomes him who undertakes so to explain it to others? . . . Have I a full and clear view of the analogy of faith, which is the clue to guide me through the whole? Am I acquainted with the several parts of Scripture, with all parts of the Old Testament and the New? Upon the mention of any text, do I know the context, and the parallel places? . . . Do I know the scope of each book, and how every part tends thereto? Have I the skill to draw the natural inferences deducible from each text? (2) Do I understand Greek and Hebrew? Otherwise . . . am I not at the mercy of everyone who does understand, or pretends to understand, the original? For which way can I confute his pretence? Do I understand the language of the Old Testament? Critically? At all? Can I read into English one of David's Psalms; or even the first chapter of Genesis? Do I understand the language of the New Testament? Am I a critical master of it? Have I enough of it even to read into English the first chapter of St. Luke? If not, how many years did I spend at school? How many at university? And what was I doing all those years?[34]

Wesley says similar things about the indispensability of knowledge of the Christian tradition. But the basic point should be clear: important elements of what we now call "analytic theology" have deep roots in the broad Christian theological tradition. Indeed, for an evangelist like John Wesley, this is simply the kind of theology that any Christian minister should be doing.

WHAT ANALYTIC THEOLOGY ISN'T: MISUNDERSTANDINGS AND OBJECTIONS

Many systematic theologians are suspicious of analytic theology. Indeed,

---

[33]Ibid., pp. 491-92.
[34]Ibid., pp. 490-91.

some are *deeply* suspicious. The concerns come from several angles. Here are some of the most common.[35]

"*Analytic theology relies on a univocal account of religious language.*" Some theologians may worry that the current analytic discussions proceed with an unrealistic and unhealthy naiveté regarding the nature and function of religious language. For instance, Stephen R. Holmes thinks that "analytic discussions of the Trinity seem generally to proceed with a remarkable confidence about the success of language in referring to the divine"; he thinks that the assumption of analytic theology "would always seem to be that language refers univocally to the divine and the created." Indeed, he thinks that analytic theology would be "impossible" without a commitment to univocity.[36] More worrisome, the concern may be that analytic theology's commitment to univocity implicates it in something that is (at least potentially) idolatrous.[37]

A general treatment of religious language is beyond the scope of our discussion, but several observations may be helpful. First, it should be noted that the case *against* univocity should not be merely assumed (as if some particular theological proposal could be damned by nothing more than the charge of univocity). Nor is the case *for* univocity nearly so weak as is often supposed. To the contrary, univocity has serious and sophisticated defenders today, and a case can be made that "the doctrine of univocity is true and salutary."[38]

The second major point is perhaps more important for our purposes. It is this: analytic theology as such requires no commitment to univocity whatsoever. Indeed, many analytic theologians reject univocity in favor

---

[35]This section draws heavily from my "Theologians, Philosophers, and the Doctrine of the Trinity," in McCall and Rea, *Philosophical and Theological Essays on the Trinity*, pp. 340-48.

[36]Stephen R. Holmes, *The Quest for the Trinity: The Doctrine of God in Scripture, History, and Modernity* (Downers Grove, IL: IVP Academic, 2012), p. 32.

[37]See, e.g., Jean-Luc Marion, *God Without Being*, trans. Thomas A Carlson (Chicago: University of Chicago Press, 1991); and John Milbank, *The Word Made Strange* (Oxford: Blackwell, 1997). See also the discussion in Daniel P. Horan, *Postmodernity and Univocity: A Critical Account of Radical Orthodoxy and John Duns Scotus* (Minneapolis: Fortress, 2014).

[38]Thomas Williams, "The Doctrine of Univocity Is True and Salutary," *Modern Theology* 21 (2005): 575-85. See also William P. Alston, *Divine Nature and Human Language: Essays in Philosophical Theology* (Ithaca, NY: Cornell University Press, 1989), pp. 17-117; and Keith E. Yandell, "Not Confusing Incomprehensibility and Ineffability: Carl Henry on Literal Propositional Revelation," *Trinity Journal* (2014): 61-74.

of other approaches (the doctrine of analogy being favored by many), and at least one prominent philosopher of religion defends apophaticism.[39] Perhaps there is a general sense in which it is true that analytic theologians are naive about religious language. *Perhaps* they are— although I doubt this very much. But even if it were true, this would not obviously make analytic theology different from or inferior to many other approaches to the theological task. The concern—even if it were substantiated—would give us no reason to avoid or dismiss analytic theology. It might give us reason to want to do it better; it might motivate analytic theologians to pay closer attention to important issues related to theological language. But the concern itself—even if substantiated— would not count against the proper exercise of analytic theology. It is, at best, a red herring.

"Analytic theology is an exercise in natural theology." Some critics might charge analytic theology with reliance on "natural theology." This observation will seem benign to other theologians; some analytic theologians might even take this judgment as a badge of honor. But to those theologians of the house and lineage of Karl Barth, this will be the mark of damnation: some may take natural theology to be "the invention of the Antichrist," as something that can serve only to reinforce idolatry and corrupt the truth.[40] Other theologians might not be so hostile, but they still might worry that natural theology distracts us from obedience and fidelity to the reality of divine revelation. So if analytic theology is an exercise in natural theology, or even relies on it, it should be held at arm's length if not shunned entirely.

Much could be said about this cluster of issues—and indeed more will be said in the next chapter—but at this point a basic confusion needs to be cleared away. Fundamentally, it is simply a misunderstanding of analytic theology to think that it is an exercise in natural theology. Granted, some prolific analytic theologians are heavily invested in the project of natural theology, and we can say with confidence that rumors of the

---

[39]E.g., Jonathan D. Jacobs, "The Ineffable, Inconceivable, and Incomprehensible God: Fundamentality and Apophatic Theology," in *Oxford Studies in Philosophy of Religion*, forthcoming.

[40]More precisely, Barth says that the *analogia entis* (which interpreters often take to be the basis of all natural theology) is the "invention of the Antichrist," *Doctrine of the Word of God*, p. xiii.

demise of natural theology have been greatly exaggerated.[41] But there is
nothing about analytic theology as such—as I have described it to this
point—that relies on natural theology. The confusion of natural theology
with the analytic project is just that—a confusion. Whatever we should
think about natural theology *philosophically*, however we judge the suc-
cesses (or lack thereof) of the various theistic arguments, natural theology simply cannot be equated with analytic theology. And whatever
we should conclude *theologically* about natural theology, we should not
confuse it with the analytic project. Once again, this is a red herring.

   "Analytic theology is naive with respect to the history of doctrine."
Another concern expressed by some contemporary systematic theologians is this: analytic theology all too often proceeds with little awareness
of the complex but important historical factors associated with the development and formation of Christian doctrine. To understate the point,
analytic theologians are sometimes criticized for their ignorance of the
history of the development of dogma and for their lack of careful study
to understand the particular intellectual (not to mention social) setting
of the person(s), controversies or eras under consideration. Instead, so
the story goes, it is all too common for analytic theologians to approach
an issue by isolating a particular text and then breaking it down to
unpack the real "core" of the doctrine in question. And the assumption
of the analytic theologians (again, so the story goes) is often enough that
this can be safely or appropriately done with little or no reference to the
particular context in which the development occurred. As Fred Sanders
expresses the concern, "philosophers sometimes seem to think of ancient
texts as cumbersome delivery systems containing ideas which it is their
job to extract from the delivery system and do something with."[42] Richard
A. Muller likewise argues that lack of attention to historical context
sometimes results in problematic misunderstandings of the tradition; in

---

[41]E.g., Richard Swinburne, *The Coherence of Theism* (Oxford: Oxford University Press, 1977); and
Swinburne, *The Existence of God* (Oxford: Oxford University Press, 1979 [2004]). For examples
of recent work, see Moreland and Craig, *Blackwell Companion to Natural Theology*; and James F.
Sennett and Douglas Groothuis, eds., *In Defense of Natural Theology: A Post-Humean Assessment*
(Downers Grove, IL: IVP Academic, 2005).

[42]Fred Sanders, "The State of the Doctrine of the Trinity in Evangelical Theology," *Southwestern
Journal of Theology* 47 (2005): 169.

his view, for instance, both recent defenders and contemporary detractors of the doctrine of divine simplicity commonly "misinterpret the
traditional doctrine."[43] Robert W. Jenson is more scathing: he judges the
analytic enterprise to be "somewhat oddly related to the Christian faith
it claims to defend," and he calls the work of Richard Swinburne a "truly
bizarre case."[44]

At least this is how the story often goes. A major underlying worry
seems to be that reading texts without proper attention to their social
location and intellectual context can cause us to misread and misinterpret those texts. This strikes me as a legitimate concern, and it is one
that analytic theologians would do well to hear and heed. No one should
deny that it is possible to misread and misinterpret important historical
texts, and it seems to me that such misreadings are far more likely when
particular bits of the text are isolated and scrutinized apart from the
broader literary and historical contexts. The temptation to look away
from the context as an irrelevant distraction is real. It should also be
resisted. So the criticism contains an important caution.

At the same time, however, we should keep several additional points
in mind. First, the problem is not restricted to analytic theologians—
constructive or systematic theologians of any stripe may be susceptible
to this temptation. Indeed, ironies abound on this front. After criticizing
analytic philosophers of religion for overlooking "the essentially historical character of trinitarian theology"—and especially for missing the
important differences between the "Greek (or 'Cappadocian') East" and
the "Latin West"—Catherine Mowry LaCugna's own work has been
criticized for *exaggerating* those differences.[45] It is not as if more mainstream, nonanalytic or antianalytic theologians are immune to the temptation; instead, so far as I can see, this is a general concern that should
serve as an important reminder that all theologians who engage with the

---

[43]Richard A. Muller, *Post-Reformation Reformed Dogmatics: The Rise and Development of Reformed Orthodoxy, ca. 1520–ca. 1725*, vol. 3, *The Divine Essence and Attributes* (Grand Rapids: Baker Academic, 2003), p. 41.

[44]Robert W. Jenson, *Systematic Theology*, vol. 2, *The Works of God* (Oxford: Oxford University Press, 1999), p. 8 n. 35.

[45]Catherine Mowry LaCugna, "Philosophers and Theologians on the Trinity," *Modern Theology* 2 (1986): 172.

Christian intellectual tradition should do so with appropriate historical sensitivity. Second, there is nothing—at least so far as I can see—that makes this temptation irresistible. The fact that some analytic theologians have been insufficiently attentive to some historical matters does not entail either that all analytic theologians are ignorant of the tradition or that all analytic theologians must proceed in ignorance. I see no reason to conclude that this problem must be either essential or endemic to analytic theology. Surely more progress can be made in this area, but I see no reasons to think that such progress cannot happen. Finally, it is worth noting that such progress in fact *is* being made. There are many happy exceptions to the common stereotype that analytic theologians are "ahistorical"; in fact, it is safe to say that many excellent analytic thinkers have genuine specialization in historical scholarship. Indeed, many are cutting-edge contributors.[46]

"Analytic theology is only apologetics for conservative theology." Alternatively, the suspicion may be that analytic theology is *too* closely tied to the Christian tradition. The assumption here is that analytic theology is nothing more than the bastion of traditionally minded Roman Catholic (and Orthodox) theologians and philosophers along with their conservative Protestant friends, and the worry is that they are interested in nothing more than finding a safe place to defend what they already know to be true. Consequently, the worry goes, there is next to nothing of real interest here for revisionist theologians of various stripes, and there is little promise for genuinely constructive theology.

Two observations are important here. First, in principle there is nothing about analytic theology that demands either traditional sympathies or conservative conclusions. Neither is there anything about analytic theology (either taken along the lines of Rea's P1-P5 or in a somewhat more expansive way) that precludes the use of the analytic tools by, say, feminist, womanist or liberationist theologies.

---

[46]Stellar examples include Richard Cross, *Duns Scotus on God* (Aldershot, UK: Ashgate, 2005); Cross, *The Metaphysics of the Incarnation: Thomas Aquinas to Duns Scotus* (Oxford: Oxford University Press, 2002); Eleonore Stump, *Aquinas* (New York: Routledge, 2003); Jeffrey E. Brower, *Aquinas's Ontology of the Material World: Change, Hylomorphism, and Material Objects* (Oxford: Oxford University Press, 2014); and J. T. Paasch, *Divine Production in Late Medieval Trinitarian Theology: Henry of Ghent, Duns Scotus, and William Ockham* (Oxford: Oxford University Press, 2012).

Second, in point of fact many criticisms of traditional doctrines have emerged from within analytic theology. Consider this example. It is hard to think of a doctrine that is more deeply traditional or more deeply woven into the fabric of historic Christian theology than the doctrine of divine simplicity. Yet this venerable doctrine has endured intense criticism from analytic theologians over the past several decades. Alvin Plantinga's *Does God Have a Nature?* raised "two difficulties" for the doctrine, "one substantial and the other truly monumental."[47] He argues that if God is identical with each of his properties, then God has but one property. But this "seems flatly incompatible with the obvious fact that God has several properties."[48] He argues further that if God is identical with each of his properties, then God is also a property. "This view is subject to a difficulty both obvious and overwhelming . . . [for] if God is a property, then he isn't a person but a mere abstract object."[49] Many analytic theologians have joined other criticisms to those of Plantinga, and it is obvious that this doctrine—woven deeply into the fabric of traditional Christian doctrine as it is—is under assault from within analytic theology. We could multiply examples with ease. (The traditional doctrine of divine omniscience stands out here.) There are, of course, many sophisticated defenders of classical orthodoxy within analytic theology, but the basic point should be clear: to reduce analytic theology to apologetics for traditional doctrine is simply a mistake.

As will become obvious in the following pages, I think that there is much to be gained in the work of "retrieval theology," and I see it as a natural conversation partner and compatriot of analytic theology. I want to encourage more work at the intersection of analytic theology and theologies of retrieval. But there is nothing about analytic theology as such that demands adherence to classical Christian theology.

"Analytic theology relies on 'substance metaphysics.'" Sometimes theologians are suspicious of analytic theology due to its alleged reliance on substance metaphysics. This complaint can take various forms. Some-

---

[47]Alvin Plantinga, *Does God Have a Nature?* (Milwaukee: Marquette University Press, 1980), p. 47.
[48]Ibid.
[49]Ibid.

times it is claimed that the whole analytic enterprise is "pre-Kantian" (as in Kenneth Surin's critique of David Brown's work as being "robustly old-fashioned" and "pre-Kantian").[50] In other words, critics complain that analytic theology proceeds in blithe—and perhaps willful—ignorance of the "fact" that Kant undermined the entire project by destroying the very possibility of doing it. Two important claims seem to be in play with this critique: first, that Kant did something to make analytic theology impossible; and second, that analytic theologians are unaware of what Kant did. But both of these claims are problematic. The second is simply mistaken, and the first is vigorously contested. As Nicholas Wolterstorff points out, it is much more likely that the current generation of analytic theologians is not so much "pre-Kantian" as it is "post-Kantian." As he puts it, "it really is possible to be post-Kantian. It's possible to recover from Kant. The choices are not exhausted between being naively pre-Kantian, on the one hand, and being a Kantian of one or another stripe, on the other."[51] There are, Wolterstorff argues, philosophers who are fully aware of Kantian "interpretation-universalism and fully aware of [Kantian] metaphysical anti-realism; but after serious consideration, they have rejected these options as untenable."[52] So many analytic theologians are well aware of Kant's work (and the common claims made about that work), but they don't think that he did anything to shut down the kind of work that they are doing. As Plantinga puts it, "they *have* read him and remain unconvinced."[53]

But aside from Kant, analytic theology is sometimes criticized and rejected for its reliance on "substance metaphysics." Unfortunately, exactly what critical theologians have in their crosshairs when they talk about substance metaphysics is often unclear and not closely defined. But very often the complaint is closely tied to a rejection of doctrines

---

[50]Kenneth Surin, "The Trinity and Philosophical Reflection: A Study of David Brown's *The Divine Trinity*," *Modern Theology* 2 (1986): 239-40.

[51]Nicholas Wolterstorff, "Between the Pincers of Increased Diversity and Supposed Irrationality," in *God, Philosophy, and Academic Culture: A Discussion Between Scholars in the AAR and APA*, ed. William J. Wainwright (Atlanta: Scholars Press, 1996), p. 20. See also Wolterstorff, "Is It Possible and Desirable for Theologians to Recover from Kant?," *Modern Theology* 14 (1998): 1-18.

[52]Wolterstorff, "Between the Pincers," p. 20.

[53]Alvin Plantinga, *Warranted Christian Belief* (Oxford: Oxford University Press, 2000), p. 30.

associated with "classical theism"; immutability, impassibility, time-lessness and other doctrines are taken to be untenable, and, since they are tied to substance metaphysics, so much the worse for substance metaphysics. William P. Alston deftly analyzes this complaint, and he argues that substance metaphysics are really beside the point. What he says about substance metaphysics in discussions of the doctrine of the Trinity applies more broadly: "once we get straight as to what is and is not necessarily included in the metaphysics of substance, we will see that most twentieth-century objections to the use of substance metaphysics . . . are based on features of such formulations that are not required by substance metaphysics as such."[54] Perhaps there is something inherently wrong with the use of substance metaphysics in theology, and maybe this counts against analytic theology. But before such a judgment can be made, we need more than the all-too-common generalizations and as-sertions. For before we can conclude that analytic theology is fatally flawed due to a dependence on substance metaphysics, we need to know exactly what is meant by substance metaphysics, we need to be shown just *what* is wrong (either philosophically or theologically) with sub-stance metaphysics and we need to see that analytic theology really is (or must be) committed to this kind of metaphysics. Without the kind of careful analysis and rigorous argumentation, it is hard to see anything here that might count as a forceful objection to analytic theology.

"Analytic theology isn't spiritually edifying." William Wood notes that "many conventional theologians remain deeply suspicious of analytic the-ology" because of the worry that analytic theology is not spiritually edi-fying. As these theologians see matters, "genuine theology is in the first instance practical: aimed not at explanatory theories about God, but at fostering greater love for God and neighbor. Genuine theology, in short, is *praxis*, one deeply woven together with a Christian life of prayer, virtue, and participation in the sacraments."[55] The basic concern is this: when more mainstream theologians look at analytic theology, they don't rec-

---

[54]William P. Alston, "Substance and the Trinity," in *The Trinity: An Interdisciplinary Symposium on the Trinity*, ed. Stephen T. Davis, Daniel Kendall, SJ, and Gerald O'Collins, SJ (Oxford: Oxford University Press, 1999), p. 201.

[55]William Wood, "Analytic Theology as a Way of Life," *Journal of Analytic Theology* (2014): 44.

ognize the kind of theology-as-praxis that they value. Instead, they see purported explanatory theories—*mere* purported explanatory theories. Sometimes these explanations appear to be a very long way indeed from the life of faith. Indeed, they see formulas such as this (selected pretty much at random from among many others):

P: $\exists x\ (Dx\ \&\ \forall y(Dy => Byx)\ \&\ x$ made us;
Q: $\exists x(Dx\ \&\ \forall y(Dy => Byx)).$[56]

When they encounter this kind of work, some theologians don't recognize it as theology at all. If they are willing to recognize it as theology, they tend to worry that they don't see the kind of theology that promotes love of God and neighbor; they are concerned that they don't see theology that is connected to the life of faith. As Wood puts it, they worry that "analytic theology is spiritually sterile and therefore not really a form of genuine theology at all."[57]

I think this is an important point of criticism, and it raises some very intriguing concerns. But as Wood also notes, it would be a "mistake, and furthermore a presumptuous mistake, to assume that analytic philosophical theology cannot in principle be spiritually nourishing."[58] Three points stand out. First, it is important to realize that the temptation to construct explanatory theories about God that are divorced from worship and transformation is both real and present. It is also nefarious.[59] The temptation besets theologians of all stripes—analytic or otherwise. I do not think analytic theologians are the only theologians who face this temptation. To the contrary, idolatry is no respecter of ideologies. But surely it is not invincible; surely—by God's grace—it is not irresistible. As Wood reminds us, "God's love rains down on logicians too, after all."[60]

Second, there is good reason to think that analytic theology may—contrary to common expectations—turn out to be spiritually edifying.

---

[56]Peter van Inwagen, "And Yet They Are Not Three Gods but One God," in McCall and Rea, *Philosophical and Theological Essays on the Trinity,* pp. 241, 246.
[57]Wood, "Analytic Theology as a Way of Life," p. 44. See also Marilyn McCord Adams, "What's Wrong with the Ontotheological Error?," *Journal of Analytic Theology* (2014): 1-12.
[58]Wood, "Analytic Theology as a Way of Life," p. 46.
[59]See the warnings of Merold Westphal, *Suspicion and Faith: The Religious Uses of Modern Atheism* (New York: Fordham University Press, 1998).
[60]Wood, "Analytic Theology as a Way of Life," p. 47.

Wood argues that analytic theology may be spiritually beneficial in several ways. He suggests that the "concentrated attention required to read, understand, and develop very technical analytic arguments" may be conducive to the kinds of intellectual virtues and habits of mind that are spiritually beneficial.[61] In addition, he notes, the "argumentative transparency" (what he terms the "paradigmatic analytic virtue") may be helpful in spiritual formation.[62] Wood readily admits that this tendency toward argumentative rigor can also feed a form of pride or even "intellectual violence," but he also points out that to make a "good analytic argument is to make that argument maximally easy for intellectual opponents to criticize or refute," and this very transparency makes it much harder to shield oneself from criticisms but instead is a way to "make oneself intellectually vulnerable." In this way it serves as a "check against intellectual pride."[63] Moreover, the pace demanded by such rigor, and the modesty of the claims that are rendered defensible, have the potential to cultivate epistemic humility. Furthermore, another important feature of the analytic approach is the need to "identify imaginatively with one's intellectual opponents"; this also, as Wood points out, forces us to inhabit a worldview that is not only foreign to our own but also sometimes hostile. In these ways, Wood argues, "analytic theology can become a spiritual practice: a way of seeking God, and of training the mind and the will to be open to grace."[64]

Finally, we should not neglect to notice those shining examples of theologians for whom analytic theology indeed is closely related to worship and spiritual nurture. Indeed, it would be hard not to notice them, for the tradition is rife with such theologians. A great many patristic and most scholastic (both medieval and early modern) theologians count as "analytic theologians." For surely they fit our profile of theologians who prize "conceptual precision, rigor of argumentation, technical erudition, and an in-depth defense of an original worldview" (and who would, in many instances, value P1-P5). As an example, con-

---

[61]Ibid., p. 55.
[62]Ibid., p. 56.
[63]Ibid.
[64]Ibid., p. 58.

sider Anselm's *Proslogion.* It is obvious that Anselm values precision and rigor, and he clearly intends to convey truth claims that he finds convincing. But as both Wood and Marilyn McCord Adams point out, this work is "meant to do more than communicate propositional truths"; for "it is meant to help reorient the wills of its readers, and help bring about effective and volitional change in them."[65] Despite important differences of style and substance, we could say much the same about many other figures (both well known and less so) as well: it is very difficult to read far into Bonaventure, Richard of St. Victor, Aquinas, Scotus, Vermigli, Perkins, Arminius, Turretin, Edwards, Wesley and many others without understanding that they are obviously concerned with both intellectual rigor and spiritual formation.

---

[65]Ibid., p. 50. See also Marilyn McCord Adams, "Praying the Proslogion," in *The Rationality of Belief and the Plurality of Faith,* ed. Thomas Senor (Ithaca, NY: Cornell University Press, 1995), pp. 13-39; and Adams, "Elegant Necessity, Prayerful Disputation: Method in *Cur Deus Homo*," in *Studia Anselmiana: Cur Deus Homo* (Rome: 1999), pp. 367-96.

2

Analytic Theology and
Christian Scripture

So listen to my last piece of advice: exegesis, exegesis,
and yet more exegesis! Keep to the Word, to the
Scripture that has been given to us.

KARL BARTH

WHAT HATH JERUSALEM TO DO with Athens? What does
modal analysis have to do with biblical exegesis? What does the
Bible have to do with philosophical theology? In this chapter, I try to get
clearer on the relation of analytic theology to the study of the Bible as
Christian Scripture. First, I shall discuss the role and function of theological analysis as response to revelation. Here, after noting what seems
to be a great gulf fixed between analytic theology and biblical studies, I
shall clear away some misconceptions about "natural theology" and
"perfect being theology." Second, I shall consider the relation between
analytic theology and claims about the "authority" of biblical theology.
Third, through the use of an interesting case study I shall demonstrate
how biblical theology and analytic theology may be not only complementary but also mutually enriching. Throughout, I shall proceed from
the conviction that analytic theology—as Christian theology—should be
faithful to Scripture and engaged with biblical scholarship.

Epigraph: Karl Barth, in Eberhard Busch, *Karl Barth: His Life from Letters and Autobiographical
Texts* (Philadelphia: Fortress, 1976), p. 259.

ANALYTIC THEOLOGY AND THE RESPONSE TO REVELATION

Philosophical analysis and biblical exegesis: The initial distance. Analytic theology is sometimes characterized as the ultimate exercise in "armchair theology"; some theologians harbor deep suspicions that it merely engages in some highfalutin and arcane discourse about God and the world that is just, well, made up. In other words, they worry that analytic theologians bypass and effectively ignore God's own revelation as it occurs ultimately in the incarnation of the Holy Son and reliably in the Bible as Holy Scripture. Trading the glorious gift of divine revelation for the tangled mess of their own a priori theological musings, the best they can do is to wallow in their own irrelevant wonderings and wanderings. At worst, they commit conceptual idolatry.

Sometimes these suspicions are well-founded. Consider the judgment of J. L. Tomkinson when faced with biblically based objections to his proffered view of God and time: what the Bible says is simply "irrelevant to philosophical questions."[1] He continues by insisting that in the case of conflict between the conclusions of philosophical theology and the claims of revelation, "the problem . . . must always, insofar as philosophical theology is concerned, lie with the advocates of the revelation in question." For if philosophical theology "leads to a conclusion which seems at odds with revelation, the former may claim the credentials of reason" in a way that revealed theology cannot.[2] So in the case of a conflict between the claims of philosophical theology and the deliverances of revealed theology, there really is no contest: "reason" enjoys the presumption of victory over "revelation." Much could be said about Tomkinson's approach; while it is far from obvious that he is correct, there are good reasons to think that he is mistaken. As Thomas F. Torrance has argued, the mark of genuine rationality in any kind of valid scientific inquiry is to allow our approach to the subject matter to be shaped and reshaped by the reality as it is.[3] If Torrance is correct, then

---

[1]J. L. Tomkinson, "Divine Sempiternity and A-temporality," *Religious Studies* (1982): 177, quoted in Thomas V. Morris, *Anselmian Explorations: Essays in Philosophical Theology* (Notre Dame, IN: University of Notre Dame Press, 1987), p. 2.

[2]Tomkinson, "Divine Sempiternity," pp. 186-87, quoted in Morris, *Anselmian Explorations,* pp. 2-3.

[3]Torrance does this throughout his corpus, but see especially Thomas F. Torrance, *Theological*

we have good reason to be suspicious of Tomkinson's claims.[4] For if we have good reason to think that God *has* revealed himself (for the Christian, ultimately in the incarnation of the Son as Jesus the Christ and reliably in Holy Scripture), then we have very good reason to let that revelation correct our a priori conceptions of God's being and actions.

Fortunately, however, Tomkinson's approach is not at all representative of the vast majority of Christian analytic theology. Indeed, it seems both safe and important to point out that his view is exceptional enough that it serves better as a caricature than as an accurate characterization of analytic Christian theology. Still, though, there are important disciplinary differences between the kinds of work done by biblical scholars and the kinds of work done by philosophical theologians. And beyond the differences, there are remaining questions about the relation of analytic theology to historical-critical biblical studies and biblical theology.

Natural theology or revealed theology? Is analytic theology only a form of something called "natural theology"? And if so, is it not thus inherently and diametrically opposed to revealed theology? And just what *is* natural theology?

Theological opposition to natural theology is well known and widespread. As Plantinga notes in his discussion of the Reformed objection to natural theology, while "a few Reformed thinkers . . . endorse the theistic proofs," for "the most part the Reformed attitude has ranged from tepid endorsement, through indifference, to suspicion, hostility, and outright accusations of blasphemy."[5] Karl Barth's *Nein!* in debate with Emil Brunner is famous, and the echoes of it reverberated well into

---

Science (Edinburgh: T & T Clark, 1969). See also Tom McCall, "Ronald Thiemann, Thomas Torrance, and Epistemological Doctrines of Revelation," *International Journal of Systematic Theology* (2004): 148-68.

[4]Although beyond the scope of this discussion, the work of "Reformed epistemology" is relevant here. See Alvin Plantinga, *Warranted Christian Belief* (Oxford: Oxford University Press, 2000); and Kevin Diller, with a foreword by Alvin Plantinga, *Theology's Epistemological Dilemma: How Karl Barth and Alvin Plantinga Provide a Unified Response* (Downers Grove, IL: IVP Academic, 2014).

[5]Alvin Plantinga, "Reason and Belief in God," in *Faith and Rationality: Reason and Belief in God*, ed. Alvin Plantinga and Nicholas Wolterstorff (Notre Dame, IN: University of Notre Dame Press, 1983), p. 63. For a more nuanced view of how the Reformed scholastics understood the relation between "natural" and "supernatural" theology (both of which are revealed), see Richard A. Muller, *Post-Reformation Reformed Dogmatics: The Rise and Development of Reformed Orthodoxy, ca. 1520–ca. 1725*, vol. 1, *Prolegomena to Theology*, 2nd ed. (Grand Rapids: Baker Academic, 2003), pp. 270-310.

the following century. While many contemporary theologians (including some revisionist as well as traditional Protestants, along with many Catholic and Orthodox scholars) do not hold to "Barthian" commitments in theological method or reject just any theological enterprise deemed antithetical to Barthian constraints, many contemporary theologians in fact are sympathetic to Barth's views and share his worries about natural theology. So is analytic theology committed to natural theology—and thus out of bounds for theologians of the house and lineage of Barth?

But what, more precisely, are we talking about when we talk about "natural theology"? Suppose we take natural theology to be simply what James F. Sennett and Douglas Groothuis describe when they say that it is "the attempt to provide rational justification for theism using only those sources of information available to all inquirers, namely, the data of empirical experience and the dictates of human reason . . . [a] defense of theism without recourse to purported special revelation."[6] In this sense, natural theology is what Plantinga calls "the attempt to prove or demonstrate the existence of God."[7] Taken this way, "natural theology" really is a philosophical project; as Sennett and Groothuis say, "the term 'natural theology' is actually a misnomer. The enterprise, so conceived, is an exercise in philosophical, not theological, inquiry."[8]

Taken this way, philosophers and theologians alike have criticized the project of natural theology. Especially since David Hume's *Dialogues Concerning Natural Religion* (and *An Inquiry Concerning Human Understanding*), philosophers have debated the merits and demerits of the various traditional arguments for the existence of God. In addition to the broader discussions, they have also debated the strengths and weaknesses of Hume's own arguments—and here the verdict looks very weak for Hume's case.[9] But thus construed, what is the relation of analytic

---

[6]James F. Sennett and Douglas Groothuis, introduction to *In Defense of Natural Theology: A Post-Humean Assessment*, ed. James F. Sennett and Douglas Groothuis (Downers Grove, IL: IVP Academic 2005), p. 10.

[7]Plantinga, "Reason and Belief in God," p. 63.

[8]Sennett and Groothuis, introduction, p. 10 n. 6.

[9]Keith E. Yandell concludes that "the idea that Hume dealt a deathblow to natural theology is sheer fiction," "David Hume on Meaning, Verification, and Natural Theology," in Sennett and Groothuis, *In Defense of Natural Theology*, p. 81. Cf. Keith E. Yandell, *Hume's "Inexplicable*

theology to natural theology? The answer, frankly, is that there isn't much of one, and there isn't necessarily one at all. Analytic theology, as I have characterized it here, simply is not committed to this type of exercise. Analytic theologians may be interested in natural theology, and they may find, say, the cosmological or teleological arguments to be sound. They may even think that such work is helpful or even obligatory in apologetics. Or they may not—they may think that Barth was entirely right or maybe even understated. The point here is that natural theology—construed in this way—is not essential to the project of analytic theology. Whatever its own philosophical merits and demerits, whatever its own theological strengths and liabilities, natural theology simply is beside the point. Further discussion of it only serves to foster confusion.

Suppose we take natural theology in a related but somewhat different sense. Suppose we take it to be something more like the attempt to gain some knowledge about the nature, character and actions of God apart from special revelation. So on this construal, when Charles Taliaferro says that natural theology "is the practice of philosophically reflecting on the existence and nature of God independent of real or apparent divine revelation or scripture," what we are really interested in here is the "*and nature of God*" part.[10] It is this element—this effort to learn something about God's nature apart from God's revelation in the incarnate Word and the written Word—that is most troubling to many theologians, and gives rise to the "suspicion, hostility, and outright accusations of blasphemy." To some theologians, the relationship between revealed theology and natural theology can only rightly be described as a cage fight to the death. According to them, we are faced with the starkest of choices: either natural theology or revealed theology—and thus either arrogance and idolatry or humility and obedience. So if analytic theology is only a dressed-up version of natural theology, then so much the worse for analytic theology.

But is it true that analytic theology is only a dressed-up version of

---

Mystery": His Views on Religion (Philadelphia: Temple University Press, 1990); and John Earman, *Hume's Abject Failure: The Argument Against Miracles* (New York: Oxford University Press, 2000).
[10]Charles Taliaferro, "The Project of Natural Theology," in *The Blackwell Companion to Natural Theology*, ed. William Lane Craig and J. P. Moreland (Oxford: Blackwell, 2012), p. 1.

natural theology? And if it is, do the dire results necessarily follow? Three main points stand out in response. First, as I pointed out in the preceding chapter, there is no good reason to think that analytic theology must be committed to this kind of natural theology. If conceptual precision, rigor of argumentation, technical erudition and an in-depth defense of an original worldview (see Smith) are the hallmarks of analytic excellence, then there simply is no reason to think that the only way to attain these hallmarks is through natural theology. There is nothing about the "style and ambition" (see Rea) of analytic theology that commits it to natural theology. A "Barthian analytic theologian" could be every bit as much an analytic theologian as a "natural analytic theologian."

However, it isn't so obvious that the analytic theologian should be committed to this Barthian stance at all. As I have said, a Barthian version of analytic theology is possible. But it isn't at all obvious that it is necessary. For while there is an important distinction between "natural" and "revealed" theology, it isn't so obvious that there is a sharp bifurcation or rigid divide. This Barthian position (which we can call "extreme Barthianism") insists that all natural theology is contrary to revealed theology. But as James Barr and others have shown, this is an overstatement and overcorrection. Barr thinks that the "the absoluteness and rigidity displayed" by Barth in the conflict with Brunner "were ridiculous,"[11] he charges Barth with disastrously confusing theological and political matters (in linking "natural theology" so tightly to National Socialism), and he insists that Barth's extravagant claims are "simply preposterous."[12] "What if," Barr asks, "scripture itself sanctions, permits, evidences, or in some other way depends upon natural theology or something like it?"[13] If it does, he argues, then the Barthian argument "falls to pieces: the Word of God, as attested in the scriptures, must then *include* natural theology as part of revelation, or as the background to it, or as an implication of it or mode through which it is communicated."[14] Barth, he contends, presumes what in actuality needs argument; Barth

---

[11]James Barr, *Biblical Faith and Natural Theology* (Oxford: Clarendon, 1993), p. 19.
[12]Ibid., p. 9.
[13]Ibid., p. 19.
[14]Ibid., p. 20.

assumes that the authority of revelation implies the denial of natural theology. But since this is the very issue at stake, then this assumption is question-begging.

Barr then mounts an extensive case (especially from such texts as Acts 17; Rom 1–2; and Ps 19; 104; 119) that the Bible actually "does imply something like natural theology."[15] Scripture surely warns us of the dangers of idolatry, but again and again we are faced with evidence that the Bible does not seem at all opposed to all insights gained from natural revelation. Barth, at least as Barr reads him, has tried to pit the revealed theology of the Bible against natural theology. But, Barr argues, the Bible itself presupposes something like natural theology and interweaves it with "revealed theology." Barr finally concludes that "Barth's rejection of natural theology was never really based on biblical exegesis, nor, as he himself, at least partially, admitted, was it really representative of Protestant tradition" but was instead grounded in "trends and developments in modern theology, philosophy, and society."[16] Barr is convinced that his critique of Barth here is nothing short of "devastating" to "Barth's total theological position."[17] Whether or not Barr is right about the effect of his critique or the extent of the devastation, he has raised a serious challenge to those theologians who would dismiss natural theology on the grounds that it is diametrically and essentially opposed to revealed theology.[18] For aside from the triumphalist tone of his polemics against Barth, he has demonstrated that one cannot simply cite Barth on the conflict between natural and revealed theology and thereby assume that natural theology is mistaken and idolatrous.

Indeed, even Barth—at least the mature Barth—might not have been an "extreme Barthian." Keith L. Johnson argues that Barth's theological development, which was significant, "occurs as a series of internal adjust-

---

[15]Ibid., p. 103.

[16]Ibid. He further says that "Barthianism was an ingenious interweaving of elements that were older, whether biblical or Reformational, with elements that were entirely modern, novel, or innovational. Conceptions entirely modern, related to existentialism, to atheism, to Hegelianism, were cleverly compounded with biblical exegesis and Reformational formulae," p. 117.

[17]Ibid., p. 103.

[18]As Mike Rea has pointed out to me, Barr does not seem to consider adequately the importance of Barth's understanding of divine hiddenness. Neither is it completely obvious that Barth bases this account on the Bible (rather than revelation itself).

ments in four stages along a single christological trajectory."[19] What Barth is consistently opposed to is the kind of natural theology that allows "abstract ideas to be imported into the doctrine of God, undermining God's particular revelation in Christ and opening the door to precisely the kind of human subjectivity that he had long opposed" and found so dangerous.[20] But this does not mean that Barth remains opposed to *all* insights gleaned from natural revelation; to the contrary, Barth agrees with Aquinas that "God is revealed in and through the created order and that theologians can and should incorporate insights derived from this natural revelation into the church's theology."[21] Barth is deeply concerned about human finitude, and he is even more exercised to insist that human reason "has been so twisted by sin that the human inevitably attempts to transform the revelation she receives into an idol."[22] Indeed, the problem is so bad that "humans cannot come to accurate knowledge of God through other sources [beyond God's self-revelation in Christ], because sin has left them unable to receive or interpret this revelation without distorting it."[23] Nonetheless, there is still a proper place for genuine knowledge of God through creation. This is, however, a distinctly *christological* knowledge of God, for "Jesus Christ is determinative not only for human salvation but for all correct knowledge of God."[24] So what we have from the mature Barth, on this reading, is a distinctly *supralapsarian* version of natural theology. Because the triune God eternally covenants to be God only in relation to creation *as God is incarnate in Christ*, nature is "taken, lifted, assumed, and integrated into the actions of God's self-giving and self-declaring . . . and therefore to the world made by him."[25] So on what we might call "Barthian supralapsarian natural theology," we should conclude that "the proper content

---

[19]Keith L. Johnson, "A Reappraisal of Karl Barth's Theological Development and His Dialogue with Catholicism," *International Journal of Systematic Theology* (2011): 1.

[20]Ibid., p. 19.

[21]Keith L. Johnson, "Natural Revelation in Creation and Covenant," in *Thomas Aquinas and Karl Barth: An Unofficial Catholic-Protestant Dialogue*, ed. Bruce L. McCormack and Thomas Joseph White, OP (Grand Rapids: Eerdmans, 2013), p. 129.

[22]Ibid., p. 142.

[23]Ibid.

[24]Ibid., p. 145.

[25]Karl Barth, *Church Dogmatics*, vol. IV/3.1, *The Doctrine of Reconciliation*, ed. T. F. Torrance, trans. Geoffrey W. Bromiley (Edinburgh: T & T Clark, 1961), p. 164.

of natural revelation is God's covenant of grace in Jesus Christ, since the created order finds its being and purpose in God's eternal plan to reconcile humanity in the person and work of Christ."[26] Creation thus really does bear witness to the "glory of God" (Ps 19:1). Non-Christians "can say true things about God" but "cannot know either *that* or *how* these things are true apart from knowledge of the covenant."[27] Christians, on the other hand, know that this is ultimately *the glory of God-made-flesh*.

So, in conclusion, suppose that "extreme Barthianism" is right; suppose that natural theology is nothing more than the devil's tool for seducing theologians into idolatry. What, then, would follow for analytic theology? What would follow is this conclusion: the analytic theologian should avoid natural analytic theology and instead should pursue extreme Barthian analytic theology. Nothing would count against analytic theology per se; a victory for extreme Barthianism would not give us any reason to avoid analytic theology. On the other hand, suppose that the critics of extreme Barthianism are right that the relationship between natural theology and revealed theology is not really a death match after all. Then just what is the relationship? If there is some legitimate space for a natural theology that is truly Christian and biblically sanctioned, then what is it? This brings me to my final observation. It is simply this: on this account, there is a legitimate place for natural theology, but the analytic theologian who is also a natural theologian can allow revealed theology to clarify, correct or strengthen the insights gleaned from natural theology. Indeed, as a *Christian* theologian, the analytic theologian not only *can* but also *should* do so.

Perfect being theology and "revelational control." This discussion of natural theology brings us to consideration of the relation of what is sometimes called "perfect being theology" to analytic theology on one hand and to Christian Scripture on the other hand. Perfect being theology is sometimes taken to be the equivalent of, or as synonymous with, analytic theology. Perfect being theology is very unpopular in some theological quarters—so much so that in some contexts a theologian can accuse a theological proposal of perfect being theology, with the pre-

---

[26]Johnson, "Natural Revelation," p. 153.
[27]Ibid., p. 154.

sumption of an odious "Anselmianism," and while no one actually explains what is so odious about it, everyone is sure that being "guilty" of
it is a very bad thing indeed.[28] Not surprisingly, some theologians criticize analytic theology on the grounds that it is merely another version
of perfect being theology. But just what is perfect being theology? What
is the relation of perfect being theology to the study of the Christian
Scriptures and to biblical theology? What is said to be wrong with perfect
being theology? And what is the relation of analytic theology to it?

Anselm famously claims that God is the being "than which nothing
greater can be thought."[29] Thomas V. Morris says that Anselm's core idea
here is "best interpreted to mean that God is to be thought of as *the
greatest conceivable being*, an individual exhibiting *maximal perfection*."[30]
Accordingly, God is "a being with the greatest possible array of compossible great-making properties."[31] "A great-making property," in turn, is
defined by Morris as a property that it is "intrinsically good to have, any
property which endows its bearer with some measure of value, or
greatness, or metaphysical stature, regardless of external circumstances."[32]
An *intrinsically* good property is then further defined as those that are
"good in themselves" and so are the "proper ultimate stopping points in
explanations of goodness."[33] So on this conception, God "is thought of
as exemplifying necessarily a maximally perfect set of compossible great-
making properties."[34] In the tradition of such theological approaches,
"the Anselmian description has been understood to entail that God is,
among other things, omnipotent, immutable, eternal, and impeccable as
well as omniscient."[35]

---

[28]Jason S. Sexton, "Conclusion," in *Two Views of the Doctrine of the Trinity*, ed. Jason S. Sexton
    (Grand Rapids: Zondervan Academic, 2014), p. 213.
[29]Anselm of Canterbury, "Proslogion," in *Anselm of Canterbury: The Major Works*, ed. Brian Davies
    and Gillian Evans (Oxford: Oxford University Press, 1998), p. 87. See also Brian Leftow, "An-
    selm's Perfect Being Theology," in *The Cambridge Companion to Anselm*, ed. Brian Davies and
    Brian Leftow (Cambridge: Cambridge University Press, 2004), pp. 132-56.
[30]Thomas V. Morris, *Our Idea of God: An Introduction to Philosophical Theology* (Downers Grove,
    IL: InterVarsity Press, 1991), p. 35.
[31]Ibid.
[32]Ibid.
[33]Ibid., p. 37.
[34]Morris, *Anselmian Explorations*, p. 12.
[35]Ibid.

Perfect being theology is far from popular among mainstream constructive or systematic theologians; indeed, some theologians view it with utter disdain. For some, it isn't even worth refuting. Furthermore, it is sometimes rejected by philosophical theologians as well. But what, exactly, is so wrong with perfect being theology? Although the criticisms are varied, several stand out as especially important for our purposes.

Some critics of perfect being theology may raise concerns about the prominent role played by our intuitions. It is hard to deny that intuitions play an important role in perfect being theology. How do we make judgments—even initial, promissory and tentative judgments—about what counts as a "great-making property"? We do so by relying on our intuitions; both modal and moral (or value) intuitions are vital here. But is this not, the critics worry, to unduly elevate our own fallible and uncertain intuitions? Is it not safer and more appropriate simply to stay in the bounds of "revealed theology"?

On a closely related note, some critics charge perfect being theology with being unduly speculative. Perfect being theology, they say, encourages us to sit back and imagine what God ought to be like if God were really going to meet our standards of goodness. But this entire approach, they say, is exactly backward: why should we, as finite creatures, think that we might have epistemic access to the standards of divinity? Revealed theology, these critics conclude, should lead us to admit that the finite cannot comprehend the infinite. And if this is so, then finite creatures are not in a good position to speculate their way into good theology. Moreover, these critics charge, revealed theology should lead us to admit that we are not only finite but also fallen. Why should we, as fallen sinners, think that we can theologize from our own intellectual resources and come up with anything other than idolatry? And if this is so, then all we can do is repent of our speculation and hope for the renewal of our minds. To summarize the complaint, critics will insist that genuine knowledge of God comes always and only by the word of God, and that when that word of God comes, it teaches us to turn from our speculation about great-making properties, to question or deny our intuitions and to seek humbly for genuine knowledge of God where God has revealed himself.[36]

These concerns are important, and I think that perfect being theologians would do well to take them seriously and learn some important lessons from them. But several points stand out in response. First, intuitions—modal and moral—seem inescapable. Yes, we are limited by our creaturely finitude, and we should remember that our intuitions may be flawed and in need of correction. Yes, they (or at least some of them) are deeply influenced by societal and cultural norms, and we would be foolish to fail to recognize this or to assume that all of our intuitions are universal. Yes, they are tainted by sin, and they may seduce us into conceptual idolatry. But we have them nonetheless, and surely it is better to recognize them and name them as such than it is to ignore them or to pretend that they are operative only in our theological opponents. In fact, this is one place (among others) where the intentional transparency that is central to the analytic approach may be of help. Neither am I certain that we should always think of our intuitions *only* with suspicion; if we are designed by God to have them, then we should be grateful for them and treat them as evidence.

Furthermore, it seems plain that we rely on such intuitions in everyday biblical interpretation. We read in Scripture that God is a "Rock" (Ps 92:15); sometimes we are told that God *has become* my Rock (Ps 94:22). Christian theologians have disagreed and argued about many things, but orthodox Christians have *never*—so far as I know—divided themselves into parties, sects or denominations called "Basaltic Theologians" or "Granitic Theologians." No one argues about *when* God turned himself into a mass of granite. In fact, the idea that anyone might do so rightly strikes us as preposterous. Why? Because all Christians agree that proper biblical interpretation should lead us to conclude that such texts should not be understood *literalistically.* But why not? Why shouldn't they be interpreted this way? Such texts don't come color-coded in the most ancient Hebrew manuscripts in shades that tell us "do not interpret this passage literalistically." But we do not *need* such hints or helps to know that we need not and should not draw such theological conclu-

---

[36]For a forceful expression of this complaint, see Bruce L. McCormack, "Seek God Where He May Be Found: A Response to Edwin Chr. van Driel," *Scottish Journal of Theology* (2007): 62-79.

sions. Neither do we need a sophisticated course of study in herme-neutics to know this. I think that the reason we do not is fairly plain: our intuitions about God tell us this much. And perhaps the explanation goes deeper—maybe we were created with the capacity for such thoughts and the development of such intuitions.

So with respect to our intuitions about great-making properties, we can recognize them and even be grateful for them while also cheerfully admitting our finitude and readily admitting our fallenness. Accordingly, we can do our best to hold our intuitions humbly and seek earnestly to have them corrected and reset in light of God's self-revelation of his own standards. Indeed, we not only can seek to do so but also *should* do so. But at any rate, it seems that our intuitions are inescapable, and it appears that they keep leading us to perfect being theology. Even Jürgen Moltmann, who is rightly known as a vociferous critic of classical theology, argues from his intuitions about divine perfection to his conclu-sions about the necessity and eternality of creation: "A non-creative God would be imperfect compared with the God who is eternally creative."[37] So it seems clear: our intuitions are inescapable, and it seems far better to bring them into the open and allow them to be corrected in light of revelation than to pretend that they are not there (or to pretend that only perfect being theologians employ them).

My second observation is this: it seems hasty and mistaken to con-clude that perfect being theology is always or necessarily at odds with revealed theology. It is true that perfect being theology is supported by the modal (S5) ontological argument, for according to this argument, if God exists, then God exists necessarily and as necessarily exemplifying maximal greatness.[38] But the support for perfect being theology is not limited to "natural theology." To the contrary, the Christian Scriptures at

---

[37]Jürgen Moltmann, *The Trinity and the Kingdom: The Doctrine of God* (Minneapolis: Fortress, 1993), p. 106.

[38]E.g., Alvin Plantinga, *The Nature of Necessity* (Oxford: Clarendon, 1974), pp. 197-219; Robert E. Maydole, "The Ontological Argument," in Craig and Moreland, *Blackwell Companion to Nat-ural Theology*, pp. 553-92. E. J. Lowe's version of the ontological argument yields a less robust theology, but he nonetheless concludes that it has a "close affinity with St. Anselm's original argument," "A Modal Version of the Ontological Argument," in *Debating Christian Theism*, ed. J. P. Moreland, Chad Meister and Khaldoun A. Sweis (New York: Oxford University Press, 2013), p. 70.

least point us in this direction. Consider such texts that exult in divine greatness: "Great is the LORD, and most worthy of praise" (Ps 48:1), or that ask "who is like the LORD?" (Ps 89:6). Such texts testify to God's incomparable greatness. Or consider what the author of Hebrews says: "When God made his promise to Abraham, since there was no one greater for him to swear by, he swore by himself, saying, 'I will surely bless you and give you many descendants'" (Heb 6:13-14; see Gen 22:16).[39] The text makes it clear: *there was no one greater for him to swear by.* It then adds this commentary: "People swear by someone greater than themselves, and the oath confirms what is said and puts an end to all argument" (Heb 6:16). Clearly, for the author of Hebrews, God is the greatest being. Furthermore, for the author of Hebrews, God himself knows that he is the greatest being. So God knows of no one greater than himself—and, even though this does not get us all the way to the conclusion that God is the greatest *conceivable* being, it is certainly consistent with it. What is the "biblical" alternative—*imperfect* being theology? Morris is convinced that "the conception of God as unsurpassably great is clearly a central biblical idea."[40] I take it that he has good reason to think this. Minimally, it seems safe to conclude that a strong case can be made for the compatibility of perfect being theology and revealed theology. For as the psalmist puts it,

> Great is the LORD and most worthy of praise;
> *his greatness no one can fathom.* (Ps 145:3)[41]

If indeed there is a proper place for perfect being theology, then just what is that place? How should the conclusions of perfect being theology—especially when motivated by our fallible intuitions and fueled by our speculation—relate to revealed theology? Ronald J. Feenstra asks some important questions. "How should Christians formulate their concept of God? What status should be accorded to Anselmian views of

---

[39]I owe this insight to Paul Helm, "Perfect Being Theology," *Helm's Deep: Philosophical Theology* (blog post), October 1, 2010, http://paulhelmsdeep.blogspot.com/2010/10/perfect-being-theology.html.

[40]Morris, *Our Idea of God*, p. 35.

[41]Yoram Hazony, on the other hand, is a Jewish analytic theologian who does not find anything like the perfect being theology of Anselm in Scripture, *Philosophy of Hebrew Scripture: An Introduction* (Cambridge: Cambridge University Press, 2012).

God, or concepts of God rooted more broadly in natural theology?"[42] Feenstra doesn't reject perfect being theology, but he does offer this important word of caution: "If Christians use Anselmian methods to articulate their concept of God, they must use these methods only insofar as they reflect what Scripture says about God. And if there is any conflict between the deliverances of Scripture and the deliverances of the Anselmian method, Christian theologians should favor what Scripture says."[43] Ultimately, of course, Scripture points us to Jesus Christ; the written Word points us to the living and incarnate Word. Accordingly, Christian theology should always seek to conform itself to God's self-revelation in the incarnation of the Son.

Feenstra asks the crucial question: "By what method, then, should Christian theologians develop their understanding of God's attributes?" He answers that Scripture itself leads us to Anselmian reflection, but that these Anselmian reflections must always be revisable in light of God's most direct revelation (ultimately in the incarnation of the Son of God, and reliably in Christian Scripture). I quote in extenso:

> The place to start, of course, is Scripture, which describes God as unsurpassably great, powerful, all-knowing, sovereign over all creation (that is, not confined to certain localities), without beginning of days or end of life, dependent for existence on no one outside God, creator of every non-divine being, perfectly good, supremely just, and more loving than the most gracious father or mother. Anselm offers a helpful principle by which to express such attributes: God is that than which nothing greater can be thought. The Anselmian method, then, is to attribute to God great-making properties, that is, properties that it is better to have than to lack, and then to say that God has these properties to a superlative degree. So in an attempt to summarize the biblical depiction of God, Anselmian theology describes God as the greatest possible being who possesses great-making properties such as maximal power (omnipotence), knowledge of every truth (omniscience), and perfect goodness. But Anselm's method can only be a guide, not the final word.[44]

---

[42]Ronald J. Feenstra, "A Kenotic Christological Method for Understanding the Divine Attributes," in *Exploring Kenotic Christology: The Self-Emptying of God*, ed. C. Stephen Evans (Oxford: Oxford University Press, 2006), p. 158.

[43]Ibid., p. 162.

[44]Ibid., p. 163.

What this means is that while perfect being theology has a legitimate and, indeed, important role in theology, it must be correctable by revealed theology. For as Morris says, "it is possible for our value intuitions to be skewed or distorted by a dominant or powerful philosophical tradition"; thus "any well-attested data from revelation should be allowed to overturn, or correct, contrary value intuitions such as these."[45] What perfect being theology needs, in other words, is what Morris calls "revelational control."[46]

My final observation, however, takes this conversation in a somewhat different direction. To this point in our discussion, I have been favorable to perfect being theology as it relates to the task of Christian analytic theology. I have pointed out at any rate that it seems unavoidable, I have suggested that perhaps we should be grateful for our intuitions about the unsurpassable greatness of God, I have urged us to be forthcoming and appropriately suspicious of these intuitions, and I have argued that we need "revelational control" over any deliverances of the Anselmian method. Perhaps this will yield a "theo-ontology" (rather then an onto-theology).[47] But it is also important to point out that perfect being theology is in no way essential to the ambitions, style or approach of analytic theology. Debates about the relative merits and demerits of perfect being theology can take place *within* analytic theology; this is an intramural discussion.

Keith E. Yandell stands as a clear and shining example of an analytic theologian who rejects perfect being theology (at least of the common, Anselmian type). Yandell contrasts what he labels "plain theism" with "Anselmian theism." For the Anselmian theologian, God exists necessarily, God exists in all possible worlds, and God exists as necessarily maximally excellent and good in all possible worlds. God is the greatest conceivable being, the one who is maximally excellent as well as necessarily existent. There are no possible worlds in which God commits sin, for God is, strictly speaking, both necessarily existent and necessarily

---

[45]Morris, *Our Idea of God*, p. 43.
[46]Ibid. Cf. Morris, *Anselmian Explorations*, p. 25.
[47]See the discussion of Kevin J. Vanhoozer, *Remythologizing Theology: Divine Action, Passion, and Authorship* (Cambridge: Cambridge University Press, 2010), pp. 93-105.

good. So on *trinitarian* Anselmian theism, all divine persons are necessarily good. And on *incarnational* trinitarian Anselmian theism, the divine person who is now incarnate for us is necessarily good as human and divine. Yandell recognizes that a broadly Anselmian view is dominant historically; he knows that this is the default position in the Christian tradition. Nonetheless, he diverges from this tradition, and in place of Anselmianism he offers "plain theism." According to plain theism, "*being divine*, Judeo-Christianly construed, includes being omnipotent and omniscient and morally perfect."[48] Of course perfect being theology agrees with this. The divergence between plain theism and perfect being theology can be seen, however, in what it means to be "morally perfect." On Yandell's account, for the perfect being theologian, moral perfection equals or at least entails necessary moral goodness. For the plain theism theorist, however, this isn't at all obvious—perhaps *moral* perfection isn't even consistent with necessity. After all, the defender of plain theism argues, there are good reasons to think that moral responsibility demands robust freedom. We shouldn't misunderstand the claim of plain theism here: it surely *isn't* the claim that God *is* less than morally perfect, it *is* the claim that God's moral perfection is logically contingent rather than necessary. Neither should we draw the wrong conclusions about plain theism. As Yandell explains, plain theism does not entail that divine goodness isn't completely *stable*.

> For all that, if [plain theism] is true, deicide is not something to worry about. For if God can know the future—in particular, can know His own future choices—He can know whether He will ever choose to sin or not. Suppose He knows He will not. So deicide will not occur. Suppose He knows he will. Then He now knows that He will sin in the future, and does nothing now to prevent that inelegance, and so is not morally perfect even now, and so has committed deicide already. So if God exists at all, and deicide is a sin, then deicide will never occur. Whatever reason we have to think that God does exist, we have the same reason to think that He will not self-destruct, whether or not [Anselmian theism] is true.[49]

---

[48]Keith Yandell, "Divine Necessity and Divine Goodness," in *Divine and Human Action: Essays in the Metaphysics of Theism*, ed. Thomas V. Morris (Ithaca, NY: Cornell University Press, 1988), p. 315.
[49]Ibid., pp. 315-16.

There is a lot more to plain theism than this brief summary might indicate, and Yandell's proposal deserves a fuller hearing than it has received in the literature to this point. But the basic point for our purposes should be clear: there is no good reason to assume that perfect being theology is essential to analytic theology. Yandell stands as an example of an analytic theologian who is *not* a perfect being theologian—at least not one who is anything close to the "Anselmian" variety.

The upshot of all this should be obvious: the analytic theologian can help herself to perfect being theology, but she need not do so in order to do genuine analytic theology. Where does this then leave us? So far as I can see, the analytic theologian can endorse and engage in perfect being theology. Embracing perfect being theology does not, contrary to some popular misconceptions, imply that the theologian must trade her birthright of revelation for a mess of tangled, uncertain and perhaps competing speculations. Of course that is always a possibility for a perfect being theologian, and she should be aware of the temptation (although it is important to see that theologians claiming to work strictly with "revealed theology" may do the same thing—and perhaps while failing to recognize or admit that this is what is happening). But the analytic theologian who sees a proper place for perfect being theology may also submit to "revelational control." Indeed, she may even happily agree with Karl Barth when he says that "who God is and what it means to be divine is something we must learn where God has revealed Himself and His nature, the essence of the divine."[50] She can heartily concur with Feenstra when he says that "if Jesus Christ is God's decisive and clearest revelation to humanity, then our understanding of God will need to be shaped by what is revealed through and by him."[51] So the analytic theologian may embrace perfect being theology; she may, with gratefulness but also with a humble openness to correction in light of revelation, recognize and utilize her intuitions about God's unsurpassable greatness. If she is faithful to God's revelation of himself and his ways as this occurs ultimately in Christ and reliably in Scripture, then her analytic theology may

---

[50]Barth, *Church Dogmatics*, IV/1:186. Cf. Feenstra, "A Kenotic Christological Understanding," p. 160.

[51]Feenstra, "A Kenotic Christological Understanding," p. 161.

be *theology*. On the other hand, the analytic theologian who is, for whatever philosophical or theological reasons, suspicious of perfect being theology may simply eschew it. For while perfect being theology is a natural and historic ally of analytic theology, it is not essential to it.

BIBLICALLY "AUTHORIZED" ANALYTIC THEOLOGY?

Analytic theology—whether occurring as "natural analytic theology," "perfect being analytic theology," "Barthian analytic theology" or as some eclectic combination—needs "revelational control" if it is to be genuine Christian theology. So for Christians who think that God has revealed himself ultimately in the incarnation of the Son and reliably in Scripture (which itself points us to God's self-revelation in Christ), adherence to the biblically revealed and christologically normed unveiling of God will be of paramount importance. Consistency with God's own revelation of himself and his ways will be crucial.

But what does it mean to say that some theological proposal is "authorized" by revelation? It is an astounding and humbling thing for the theologian to claim, but just what does it mean? It is easy to say that some view is "biblical"—and just as easy to castigate it as "unbiblical." But what does this really mean? How is some proffered theological proposition *P* really "authorized" by scriptural teaching (for those who accept the authority of the Christian revelation)? Consider the differences between[52]

RA1 The Bible, properly (and theologically) interpreted, contains sentences that (assert propositions that) explicitly assert *P*.[53]

RA2 The Bible, properly interpreted, contains sentences that entail *P*.

RA3 The Bible, properly interpreted, contains sentences that are consistent with *P* and suggest *P*.

RA4 The Bible, properly interpreted, contains sentences that do not entail ~*P*

---

[52]I am grateful to Stephen T. Davis for stimulating me to think in this way, and for providing a model. See his "Is Kenosis Orthodox?," in Evans, *Exploring Kenotic Christology*, pp. 126-27.

[53]I say "properly (and theologically) interpreted" because even theologians who take a "traditional" view of Scripture (that it is or expresses or contains divine revelation) also realize that the Bible contains claims about God and the world that are not to be considered true but are to be judged false (think of the serpent's claim in Gen 3:4 that "you shall not certainly die").

(or some Q that is inconsistent with P), and is consistent with P (but does not suggest P; merely is neutral with respect to P).

RA5 The Bible, properly interpreted, contains sentences that entail neither P nor $\sim P$ but suggests some Q that is inconsistent with P.

RA6 The Bible, properly interpreted, contains sentences which entail $\sim P$.

RA7 The Bible, properly interpreted, clearly contains sentences which assert $\sim P$.

RA8 The Bible, properly interpreted, includes sentences that assert P, and it includes sentences that assert $\sim P$ (i.e., the Bible, even properly interpreted, is contradictory).

Clearly, some theological claim that enjoys RA1 or RA2 is in good standing for any theologian who accepts anything close to a recognizably traditional Christian doctrine of revelation. And just as clearly, any proposal that can be shown to run afoul of RA7 or RA6 will be judged to be fatally flawed. Or, if this seems too clumsy, one can simply think in terms of the distinctions between some theological claim that is *demanded by Scripture, consistent with Scripture* or *inconsistent with Scripture*. The important point is to see that there are important distinctions here, and especially that carefulness is in order in any theological work that seeks to exhibit the virtues of analytic theology while also being faithful to divine revelation. Perhaps a case study on an issue of perennial interest, as this issue has been handled in "biblical theology" (of fairly recent vintage) will be helpful. So it is to this that we now turn.

"YOU INTENDED IT FOR EVIL": BIBLICAL THEOLOGY AND THE CASE FOR COMPATIBILISM AS A CASE STUDY

Issues related to divine sovereignty and providence, on one hand, and human freedom and responsibility, on the other hand, have been of perennial interest for Christian theologians. Various proposals have been developed, criticized and refined over the centuries. Thomists and Molinists, Calvinists and Arminians, Socinians and Lutherans, and countless others besides have debated these issues. Recently, however, perspectives from "biblical theology" have promised to bring a decisive end to these debates.

Before proceeding, we should note that the term *biblical theology* can denote different things. At a very basic level, it can simply refer to any theology that seeks to be consistent with what the Bible says about God and the world. It can also mean theology that closely reflects the biblical canon in both content and shape, theology that reflects the big themes as these are developed in the canonical narrative. As Kevin J. Vanhoozer describes it,

> Biblical theology is that approach which describes the "word views" and literary shapes of the Bible, and especially as that "thick" description of the canon as a divine communicative act. Biblical theology is a description of the biblical texts on levels that display their theological significance: an integrative approach to the Bible informed by Christian doctrine. The biblical theologian reads for the theological message communicated by the texts taken individually and as a whole collection.[54]

As such, as D. A. Carson points out, it "seeks to uncover and articulate the unity of *all* the biblical texts taken together, resorting primarily to the categories of those texts themselves."[55]

Both biblical theology and analytic theology are concerned with coherence. As Alan Padgett points out, systematic theology "seeks to present a coherent vision of God, humanity, and the world, with a special focus on our lives in relationship to God and each other."[56] Analytic theology, as a kind of systematic theology, tends especially to be concerned with a focus on logical coherence. Biblical theologians, on the other hand, tend to be especially concerned with what Padgett calls "narrative coherence"; they want to see "the way things fit together and make sense in [the canonical] story."[57] These are not, of course, contradictory accounts. Indeed, they may be complementary. The analytic theologian, as *analytic* theologian, will naturally be concerned with

---

[54]Kevin J. Vanhoozer, "Exegesis and Hermeneutics," in *New Dictionary of Biblical Theology*, ed. T. Desmond Alexander, Brian S. Rosner, D. A. Carson and Graeme Goldsworthy (Downers Grove, IL: InterVarsity Press, 2000), p. 63.

[55]D. A. Carson, "Systematic Theology and Biblical Theology," in Alexander, Rosner, Carson and Goldsworthy, *New Dictionary*, p. 100.

[56]Alan G. Padgett, "The Trinity in Theology and Philosophy: Why Jerusalem Should Work with Athens," in *Philosophical and Theological Essays on the Trinity*, ed. Thomas McCall and Michael C. Rea (Oxford: Oxford University Press, 2009), pp. 332-33.

[57]Ibid., p. 333.

logical coherence. She will also, as an analytic *theologian*, care about narrative coherence.

Carson's case for compatibilism. D. A. Carson argues that both divine sovereignty, on one hand, and human responsibility and freedom, on the other hand, are central to the vision of reality that is depicted in the biblical narrative. Thus neither is negotiable for the Christian; it simply is not possible for Christian theology to surrender either belief in divine sovereignty or human responsibility and remain truly *Christian*. In his book *Divine Sovereignty and Human Responsibility: Biblical Perspectives in Tension*, Carson shows that the sovereignty of God is attested to in many ways in Scripture: "God is the Creator, Ruler, and Possessor of all things," God is, in some sense, "the ultimate personal cause of all that happens," God is the one who "elects his people" and God "is the unacknowledged source of good fortune or success."[58] Likewise, Carson argues that Scripture unmistakably demonstrates the reality and importance of human responsibility. Scripture does so in various ways: we see it in the presence, earnestness and urgency of divine commands and exhortations; in the biblical testimony that human persons make sinful choices and rebel against God and his commands; by the fact that these rebellious sinners face his just judgment; and by the fact that human agents are held responsible to respond properly to the divine initiative and entreaties to repent, believe and obey.[59] So both divine sovereignty and human responsibility are clearly attested to in Scripture. Accordingly, Carson argues, any theological construct or system must be able to account for both elements. Moreover, it must be able to do so in a way that is consistent with other crucial elements of doctrine that are vital to orthodox, biblical Christianity. For surely it would be utterly pointless to affirm both divine sovereignty and human responsibility while also denying, either explicitly or implicitly, a doctrine such as divine goodness. As Carson himself puts it,

---

[58]Here I borrow the helpful summary of J. P. Moreland and William Lane Craig, *Philosophical Foundations for a Christian Worldview* (Downers Grove, IL: InterVarsity Press, 2003), p. 561. Cf. D. A. Carson, *Divine Sovereignty and Human Responsibility: Biblical Perspectives in Tension* (Atlanta: John Knox, 1981), pp. 18-22.

[59]Ibid., pp. 24-35.

The Bible insists again and again on God's unblemished goodness. God is *never* presented as an accomplice of evil, or as secretly malicious. . . . "He is the Rock, his works are perfect, and all his ways are just. A faithful God who does no wrong, upright and just is he" (Deut 32:4). "God is light, and in him is no darkness at all" (1 John 1:5). It is precisely because of this that Habakkuk can say to God, "Your eyes are too good to look upon evil; you can tolerate no wrongdoing" (Hab 1:13), that he has a difficult time understanding how God can sanction the terrible devastations of the Chaldeans upon his own covenant community. Note then, that the goodness of God is an assumption, the nonnegotiable.[60]

So, on Carson's biblical theology, any adequate theology will maintain both belief in divine sovereignty and commitment to human responsibility—and it will always do so without denying or even undercutting belief in the utter goodness of God.

Carson is convinced that both of these themes (divine sovereignty and human responsibility) are central to biblical theology; he is just as convinced that the way to hold them together is by appealing to "compatibilism." Many contemporary evangelical Christians embrace compatibilism. They see it as a promising way of reconciling these twin themes. Some think that compatibilism is a possibility or perhaps even the most promising strategy, but others go further. Carson is one who goes further; indeed, he goes much further. He states forthrightly that there is "no alternative, except to deny the faith."[61] Indeed, "compatibilism is a *necessary* component to any mature and orthodox view of God and the world."[62] Carson is so exercised about this that he exclaims that the rejection of compatibilism would do nothing less than "destroy biblical Christianity."[63] So, for Carson, the biblical theology that underlies Christian orthodoxy absolutely requires commitment to compatibilism.

---

[60]D. A. Carson, *How Long, O Lord? Reflections on Suffering and Evil* (Grand Rapids: Baker Academic, 2006), p. 182. By "never," I take Carson to mean that the divine author of Scripture never presents God as the accomplice of evil.

[61]Ibid., p. 212.

[62]D. A. Carson, *The Difficult Doctrine of the Love of God* (Wheaton, IL: Crossway, 2000), p. 54. See also K. Scott Oliphint's equation of "the classic or orthodox doctrine of God" with "the Reformed understanding of God"; Oliphint follows John Frame in concluding that libertarian freedom requires the rejection of "classical Christian theism," *God with Us: Divine Condescension and the Attributes of God* (Wheaton, IL: Crossway, 2012), p. 11.

[63]Carson, *Difficult Doctrine*, p. 53.

Carson is convinced that "dozens and dozens" of passages support compatibilism.[64] In addition to those sets of texts that teach divine sovereignty and those sets of texts that establish human responsibility, there are also texts that explicitly teach both. He thinks that several are especially important in establishing his claims about the orthodoxy of compatibilism: Genesis 50:19-20; Leviticus 20:7-8; 1 Kings 8:46; Isaiah 10:5; John 10:36-37; Acts 2:23; 4:23-31; 18:9-10; and Philippians 2:12-13. Before proceeding to his case, however, it will be helpful to get clear on the definition of "compatibilism" with which Carson is working (for as we shall see, his definition is importantly different from standard uses of the term). As he sees things, compatibilism teaches that

> (DS) God is utterly sovereign, but his sovereignty never functions to mitigate human responsibility; and

> (MR) human beings are morally responsible creatures, but their moral responsibility never functions to make God absolutely contingent.

This is Carson's summary of what he means by "compatibilism."

Carson argues for compatibilism from Genesis 50:19-20. Commenting on Joseph's reply to the brothers who had sold him into slavery that "you meant evil against me, but God meant it for good," Carson concludes that Joseph "does not picture the event as wicked human machination into which God intervened to bring forth good."[65] Instead, Carson is convinced that the only way to account for this passage is by recourse to compatibilism. Carson refers to Acts 4:23-29 as "perhaps the most striking instance of compatibilism" in all of Scripture.[66] Here we read, "Indeed Herod and Pontius Pilate met together with the Gentiles and the people of Israel in this city to conspire against your holy servant Jesus, whom you anointed. They did what your power and will had decided beforehand should happen" (Acts 4:27-28). Carson calls us to "note carefully, on one hand, there was a terrible conspiracy" for which the people involved "should be held accountable." But he also reminds us that the same text teaches us that "they did what God's power and will had

---

[64]Ibid., p. 52.
[65]Ibid.
[66]Ibid., p. 53.

decided beforehand would happen."[67] Carson insists that it would be a grave mistake to see Christ's betrayal, trial and death "solely in terms of the conspiracy of the local political authorities at the time, and *not* in terms of God's plan."[68] It cannot be a mere conspiracy that resulted in the untimely and tragic death of an innocent man who was in the wrong place at the wrong time, for biblical theology makes it obvious that this was "what God's power and will had decided beforehand would happen." And these twin affirmations of both human responsibility and divine sovereignty lead us, Carson concludes, to compatibilism.

To summarize, Carson clearly believes that belief in the unalterability and reliability of divine goodness enjoys nothing short of RA1 or RA2. And he just as clearly believes that compatibilism enjoys the same status. He doesn't think that compatibilism is merely consistent with biblical theology or even suggested by it. To the contrary, biblical theology and Christian orthodoxy demand nothing less.

Compatibilism and compatibilisms: Toward clarity. It is easy to see that Carson is a forceful advocate of compatibilism, by which he means that biblical theology demands commitment to belief in both the idea that

(DS) God is utterly sovereign, but his sovereignty never functions to mitigate human responsibility; and

(MR) human beings are morally responsible creatures, but their moral responsibility never functions to make God absolutely contingent.

Carson's choice of the term *compatibilism* is interesting, and it intersects with important work in metaphysics.

Compatibilism is generally taken to be the view that *determinism* and freedom—not *divine sovereignty* and freedom—are compatible.[69] Many philosophers—and, of course, many ordinary thinkers—take determinism to be a threat to human freedom. As Robert Kane notes, "Determinist or necessitarian threats to free will have taken many historical

---

[67]Ibid.

[68]Ibid.

[69]Of course it is true that issues of freedom and responsibility are entangled in many discussions; in what follows, I largely use them roughly interchangeably (noting the distinctions between them when it is important). The primary concern in this discussion, however, is with moral responsibility.

forms—fatalist, theological, physical or scientific, psychological, social, and logical."[70] But for all the variety, there is

> a core notion running through all forms of determinism that accounts for why these doctrines appear to threaten free will. Any event is determined, according to this core notion, just in case there are conditions (e.g., the decrees of fate, the foreordaining acts of God, antecedent physical causes plus laws of nature) whose joint occurrence is (logically) sufficient for the occurrence of the event: it *must* be the case that *if* these determining conditions jointly obtain, the determined event occurs. Determination is thus a kind of conditional necessity that can be described in a variety of ways. In the language of modal logicians, the determined event occurs in every logically possible world in which the determining conditions (e.g., antecedent physical causes plus laws of nature) obtain.[71]

This seems to threaten freedom (and moral responsibility), Kane observes, because if determinism is true, then "it may seem that it would not be (a) 'up to us' what we choose from an array of alternative possibilities, since only one alternative would be possible; and it may seem that (b) the origin or source of our choices and actions would not ultimately be 'in us' but in conditions . . . over which we had no control."[72]

Widely accepted definitions are helpful here. Determinism is, in William Hasker's words, the view that "for every event which happens, there are previous events and circumstances which are its sufficient conditions or causes, so that, given those previous events and circumstances, it is impossible that the event should not occur."[73] Michael Rea puts it this way:

> Determinism is commonly defined as the thesis that there is, at any given moment, only one physically possible future. We might also put it this way: Let's say that a *world-statement* is a statement describing the complete state of the world at a particular time, that is, one that fully describes how everything *is* at that particular time but omits any truths about how things were or will

---

[70]Robert Kane, introduction to *The Oxford Handbook of Free Will*, ed. Robert Kane, 2nd ed. (Oxford: Oxford University Press, 2011), p. 4.
[71]Ibid.
[72]Ibid., p. 5.
[73]William Hasker, *Metaphysics: Constructing a Worldview* (Downers Grove, IL: InterVarsity Press, 1983), p. 32.

be. . . . Let's say that a law-statement is a statement that describes *all* of the laws of nature that hold in the world. Then determinism is the thesis that the world-statement for a time *t* together with a law-statement logically entails *every* world-statement for every time later than *t*.[74]

William Lane Craig and J. P. Moreland summarize it this way: determinism is the view that "for every event that happens, there are conditions such that, given them, nothing else could have happened. For every event that happens, its happening was caused or necessitated by prior factors such that given these prior factors, the event in question had to occur."[75] The "given them" and "given those previous events and circumstances" is very important, for not all determinism is reducible to fatalism. Determinism *simpliciter* is sometimes confused with fatalism (this is the view that, given what was true "at the beginning," nothing could have been different from the way that it in fact is), but this is unfortunate.[76] So not all versions of determinism amount to fatalism; some versions are not based on logical necessity. As Yandell explains,

> Let a tensed universal description (TUD) be an accurate statement of everything that is true in the world at a given time. Each such description should be viewed as tensed to some specific time that is specified in the description. Let LN be a correct account of all of the laws of nature, and LL be a correct account of all of the laws of logic. Then determinism holds: For any TUD tensed earlier than time t, that TUD plus LN plus LL, entails any TUD tensed to time t or later. Thus, if determinism is true, the past determines a unique future. There are logical possibilities alternative to what happens at any given time; it is simply not compatible with the laws of logic, the laws of nature, and what has happened in the past that they be realized. So they will not happen, and there is no more that we can do about that than there is we do about the laws of logic, the laws of nature, or what happened in the past.[77]

So this need not be fatalism, for "there are logical possibilities alternative to what happens at a given time." Nonetheless, on determinism

---

[74]Michael C. Rea, *Metaphysics: The Basics* (New York: Routledge, 2014), p. 152.

[75]Moreland and Craig, *Philosophical Foundations*, p. 268.

[76]Yandell argues that it is the view that every truth is a necessary truth and every falsehood is a necessary falsehood, *Philosophy of Religion: A Contemporary Introduction* (New York: Routledge, 1999), p. 306.

[77]Ibid., p. 308.

there is—given the unchangeable facts of the matter about the past—
"nothing more that we can do about" the fact that those possibilities are not
open to us than there is that we can do about the laws of logic or nature.[78]

So compatibilism is, in general, the view that human freedom and
responsibility are, or at least may be, compatible with determinism. Determinism may be true, and we may yet be free.[79] "Soft determinists" are
more confident than some of their fellow compatibilists; they believe it
is possible not only that determinism and freedom are compatible but
also that determinism is true.[80] They are, then, "compatibilists who insist
that determinism does not undermine any free will or responsibility
worth having."[81]

As attractive as (philosophical) compatibilism is, however, it has
drawn many criticisms and counterarguments. One of the most common
arguments is sometimes called "the Core Argument." Although there are
other important and powerful objections to compatibilism (and to determinism), this argument, along with another, helps us get clearer on
the variety of compatibilisms. Kevin Timpe summarizes the Core Argument as follows:

(1) Free will requires the ability to do otherwise;

(2) If causal determinism is true, then no agent has the ability to do otherwise;[82]

(3) Therefore, free will requires the falsity of causal determinism.[83]

---

[78]For the Christian theist, I take "what happened in the past" to include divine action as well as
human action and other mundane occurrences. We should not confuse this account of determinism with physical nomological determinism; it includes physical nomological determinism
but is not reducible to it.

[79]Cf. Rea, *Metaphysics*, p. 153.

[80]Richard Taylor, *Metaphysics*, 2nd ed. (Englewood Cliffs, NJ: Prentice-Hall, 1974), p. 48.

[81]Kane, introduction, p. 24. "Hard determinists," on the other hand, are determinists who are
incompatibilists; they think that determinism is true, and that the truth of determinism entails
the negation of free will.

[82]Causal determinism is to be distinguished from logical determinism (and fatalism). I take
theological determinism (the view that God is the ultimate determining agent) to be most commonly (and probably most consistently) a species of causal determinism (although perhaps
other options are possible). I worry that divine determinism (by which I mean the view that all
of God's actions are also determined) leads to modal collapse (at least when allied with other
common features of theism).

[83]Kevin Timpe, *Free Will: Sourcehood and Its Alternatives*, 2nd ed. (New York: Bloomsbury, 2013),
p. 69.

Yandell summarizes another argument. Letting TUD refer to "tensed universal description," he asks us to consider "the TUD that is tensed to the time just before the last dinosaur died"; he labels this *TUDdino*.[84] He also asks us to consider the TUD when you have a cup of coffee at three o'clock this afternoon; this is called *TUDcup*. Given this, consider

(4) *TUDdino* and LL and LN entails *TUDcup*;

(5) one is not responsible for anything that one has no control over;

(6) one has no control over anything that is entailed by what one has no control over;

(7) one is not responsible for anything that is entailed by what one has no control over (from 5, 6);

(8) you have no control over what is true in *TUDdino*;

(9) you have no control over LL;

(10) you have no control over LN;

(11) you have no control over *TUDdino and LL and LN* (from 8-10);

(12) you have no control over what *TUDdino and LL and LN* entails (from 7, 11);

(13) you have no control over *TUDcup* (from 4, 12);

(14) *TUDcup* entails that *you decide to have coffee at three*;

(15) you have no control over whether you decide to have coffee at three (from 13, 14).

These arguments, and the responses to them, are widely and hotly debated. But the major and influential responses tend to follow one of two lines.

Some compatibilists, often referred to as "classical compatibilists," reject (2) (and usually [6]). They argue that even though determinism is true, agents may still have the ability to do otherwise (in some relevant sense). John S. Feinberg is a philosophical theologian who adopts and defends this approach. He distinguishes between various senses of "can":

---

[84]Yandell, *Philosophy of Religion*, p. 310.

the "ability sense" simply refers to the power necessary to perform an action; the "opportunity sense" refers to the fact that the right circumstances must be present; the "rule consistent sense" refers to the ability to do something lawfully or acceptably. Further, there is the "ill-consequence free" sense of "can," the "authority" sense and the "reasonable" sense that guarantees the rationality and intelligibility of our actions. More controversially, there is the "conditional" or "hypothetical" sense, and here Feinberg says that "some 'can' statements can be interpreted this way, even if most cannot be."[85] More controversially yet—for now we get to the arguments between compatibilists and incompatibilists—is the "contra-causal" (or libertarian) sense of "can." Feinberg then argues that while the compatibilist cannot access the final, libertarian sense, she can embrace the other senses, with the payoff being that it is still possible for the compatibilist to say that the agent could have done otherwise *in some sense*.[86]

For all its illustrious history, however, classical compatibilism has come under heavy fire in recent years. Interestingly, it catches flak from various sides; while incompatibilists continue to criticize and reject such analysis as deeply flawed, so do many fellow compatibilists. Richard Taylor expresses the worry well:

> I could not have decided, willed, chosen, or desired otherwise than I in fact did. . . . We will then want to know whether the causes of those inner states were within my control; and so on, *ad infinitum*. We are, at each step, permitted to say "could have been otherwise" only in a provisional sense . . . but must retract it and replace it with "could not have been otherwise" as soon as we discover, as we must at each step, that whatever would have to have been different could not have been different.[87]

Hugh McCann points out that "virtually everyone whose freedom to will differently we ordinarily view as compromised" (including addicts) would, by this reckoning, "count as free."[88] Even John Martin Fischer

---

[85]John S. Feinberg, *No One Like Him: The Doctrine of God* (Wheaton, IL: Crossway, 2001), pp. 722-24.

[86]Ibid., p. 725.

[87]Taylor, *Metaphysics*, p. 49.

[88]Hugh McCann, *The Works of Agency: On Human Action, Will, and Freedom* (Ithaca, NY: Cornell University Press, 1998), p. 177, cited in Timpe, *Free Will*, p. 76.

concludes that the conditional approach "has fatal problems."[89] Of course not all classical compatibilists are convinced of the need to abandon it, but many compatibilists now look elsewhere. Even Feinberg, while convinced that such an approach might be helpful in some cases, also admits that it cannot do all the work for compatibilism.[90]

Other compatibilists have taken decidedly different routes. Rather than challenge (2), they have rejected (1) (and [5]). Many compatibilists, now rejecting classical compatibilism, follow the lead of Peter Strawson and Harry Frankfurt in taking a different direction entirely. In an extremely influential essay, Frankfurt challenged the notion that responsibility requires alternative possibilities at all.[91] Frankfurt-style counterexamples (as they are now known) attempt to demonstrate the irrelevance of alternative possibilities. These abound; David Hunt's version (employed by Feinberg) works well:

> Jones murders Smith, and does so under conditions which are as favorable as possible to Jones's freedom and responsibility, given the following peculiarity. There is a third party, Black, who wishes Jones to murder Smith, and who possesses a mechanism capable of monitoring and controlling a person's thoughts. Thinking that Jones might well do what he wishes him to do anyway, but unwilling to be disappointed in this expectation, Black programs the mechanism to monitor Jones's thoughts for evidence for his intentions with respect to murdering Smith, and to manipulate those thoughts to ensure the murder of Smith should it appear that Jones is not going to acquire the requisite intervention in any other way. As it happens, the mechanism does not have to intervene in the course of events, because Jones goes ahead and murders Smith on his own.[92]

Here is the (most) relevant point: Jones did not have any genuine alternative possibilities, for he was going to kill Smith one way or the other (whether or not Black and his mechanism intervened). But he acted freely and is responsible for the murder, so we can see that alternative

---

[89]John Martin Fischer, "Compatibilism," in John Martin Fischer, Robert Kane, Derek Pereboom and Manuel Vargas, *Four Views on Free Will* (Oxford: Blackwell, 2007), p. 50, cited in Timpe, *Free Will*, p. 76.

[90]Feinberg, *No One Like Him*, p. 722.

[91]Harry Frankfurt, "Alternate Possibilities and Free Will," *Journal of Philosophy* (1969): 829-39.

[92]Feinberg, *No One Like Him*, p. 726.

possibilities are irrelevant to matters of freedom and responsibility.

Frankfurt-style compatibilism has generated a great deal of attention, and it remains an interesting strategy. But it has also been a magnet for criticisms (especially from incompatibilists of both determinist and indeterminist varieties). Ted A. Warfield points out that "the incompatibilist should raise at least three worries about this argument."[93] First, closer inspection shows that there really are alternative possibilities in such stories: perhaps there is only one possible *outcome*, but there are various means to that end and various possible versions of the story of Smith's murder. Second, such scenarios say nothing about determinism—even if it turns out there are no alternative possibilities. Third, it isn't at all clear that freedom and moral responsibility are all that closely linked in such scenarios.[94] Laura Waddell Ekstrom points out that one need not conjure up such elaborate scenarios to see the basic point that alternative possibilities as narrowly construed are not necessary for freedom and responsibility. After all, if someone deliberately jumps into a pit from which he cannot climb in order to avoid fulfilling his promise to help his brother clean the yard, then he is responsible for failing to fulfill his promise—even though it is not now possible for him to clean the yard. She notes that

> the question to ask is whether proponents of Frankfurt-type cases are assuming that causal determinism is true in the scenarios. If so, then the counterfactual intervener is *superfluous*, for agents in deterministic scenarios cannot do otherwise than act just as they do and could not ever have acted otherwise. It is a mistake, then, for the libertarian to grant that the agent in a Frankfurt-type scenario is responsible; one ought to remain agnostic until the metaphysical presuppositions of the example are made explicit. And for the compatibilist to assume that the agent in question is morally responsible under the assumption of determinism is question-begging in a context in which the relation between moral responsibility and alternative possibilities is at issue.[95]

---

[93]Ted A. Warfield, "Compatibilism and Incompatibilism," in Kane, *Oxford Handbook of Free Will*, p. 620.

[94]Ibid., pp. 620-21.

[95]Laura Waddell Ekstrom, "Libertarianism and Frankfurt-Style Cases," in Kane, *Oxford Handbook of Free Will*, p. 311.

So on one hand, scenarios that assume determinism both cloud the issue by introducing superfluity and beg the question. Taken on the assumption of indeterminism, on the other hand, these scenarios pose no threat to the libertarian; if Smith is controlled by the outside controller, then the libertarian can still maintain that he is not free or responsible, while if Smith does so without such control then he acts freely and responsibly. And if the controller is "global," then it is still hard to see how Smith could be held responsible for anything he does. Of course it may be that alternative possibilities are not necessary for responsibility narrowly conceived (as illustrated by the example of the boy in the pit), but if there are no morally significant alternative possibilities at some point, then it is hard to see just how the agent is responsible for what he does or for who he has become.

If Ekstrom is representative of one type of response to Frankfurt-style compatibilism, then Eleonore Stump serves up an example of Warfield's second worry.[96] She recognizes that much recent work in defense of indeterminism has held both (1) that an act is free if the decision is not causally determined and (2) that an act is free if the agent has alternative possibilities before her. Following Thomas Aquinas (and, on one interpretation, Augustine), she agrees that Frankfurt-style counterexamples show that alternative possibilities are not necessary for freedom and responsibility. But she also follows Aquinas in insisting that determinism *is* incompatible with freedom and responsibility. In other words, such scenarios demonstrate an important point, but they do nothing to show that determinism is compatible with freedom and responsibility. Neither, of course, do they show that determinism is true.

Indeed, the worries with both classical compatibilism and Frankfurt-style compatibilism are so deep and serious that even some staunch allies of (soft) determinism are looking for other options. John Martin Fischer accepts the force of Warfield's third criticism. He thus turns to a defense of what he calls "semi-compatibilism": he admits that the project of reconciling determinism with *freedom* is difficult and may turn out to be impossible—but then argues that what Frankfurt-style cases show is that

---

[96]E.g., Eleonore Stump, *Aquinas* (New York: Routledge, 2003), pp. 277-306.

moral responsibility may be compatible with determinism.[97]

Taking stock. So Carson, as a biblical scholar and theologian, insists that biblical theology and Christian orthodoxy demand compatibilism. At the same time, discussion of compatibilism flourishes in metaphysics. Meanwhile, there is precious little crossover and genuinely interdisciplinary engagement here. So just how are they related?

The first observation is the most obvious: Carson's "compatibilism" is not compatibilism as compatibilism is commonly understood. As Carson lays it out, compatibilism is the view that

> (DS) God is utterly sovereign, but his sovereignty never functions to mitigate human responsibility; and

> (MR) human beings are morally responsible creatures, but their moral responsibility never functions to make God absolutely contingent.

These two propositions are not only compatible with one another but indeed are both true. But this is not the same thing as the view that *determinism*, on one hand, and *freedom and responsibility*, on the other, are compatible. Unless one begs the question entirely by assuming that sovereignty (or, perhaps, "utter sovereignty") equals or entails determinism, these definitions are so different that the biblical support Carson adduces for "compatibilism" cannot even count as "proof" of compatibilism (when it is understood in its properly metaphysical sense). Not only does the case from biblical theology not prove the truth of compatibilism (in the sense of establishing something like RA1 or RA2); it doesn't so much as support it. For as soon as we compare Carson's definition of compatibilism with standard definitions, we can see that we simply aren't talking about the same thing. So when he claims that "compatibilism is a *necessary* component to any mature and orthodox view of God and the world," this claim does not support the conclusion that holding to both *determinism and freedom* is a necessary component of any mature and orthodox view of God and the world.[98] The conjunction of (DS) and (MR) are consistent with various indeterminist proposals too. And when

---

[97]E.g., John Martin Fischer, "Frankfurt-Type Examples and Semicompatibilism: New Work," in Kane, *Oxford Handbook of Free Will*, pp. 243-65.
[98]Carson, *Difficult Doctrine*, p. 54.

he says that the rejection of "compatibilism" would "destroy biblical Christianity," he shouldn't be taken to mean that the rejection of the thesis that *determinism and freedom are compatible* results in the destruction of biblical Christianity.[99] Despite the fact that he says that his view is "sometimes called *compatibilism*" in "the realm of philosophical theology," it simply isn't.[100] Carsonian "compatibilism" and metaphysical compatibilism are not identical.

But Carson's arguments from biblical theology are often taken to be supportive of genuine compatibilism, and his own views of the metaphysics are not entirely clear.[101] Some theologians appeal to his work as decisive support for metaphysical compatibilism.[102] Some philosophers and apologists do as well.[103] So consider again Carson's argument from Genesis 50:19-20. As we have seen, Carson is convinced that the only way to read this passage is by recourse to compatibilism, and he concludes that Joseph "does not picture the event as wicked human machination into which God intervened to bring forth good."[104] The text does not "picture God as *post eventu* deflecting the evil action of the brothers and transforming it into something good."[105] Supposing that this argument is to be taken as supportive of metaphysical compatibilism, what should we make of it? Surely, it *is* "wicked human machination" on the part of

---

[99]Ibid., p. 53.

[100]Ibid., p. 52.

[101]Carson rejects what he calls "absolute power to contrary" in favor of John Calvin's notion of a free action as that which is "voluntary," *Divine Sovereignty*, p. 208. "On biblical grounds," he does "not think that notions of human freedom which entail absolute power to contrary can be maintained," p. 209. He is also quite dismissive of Alvin Plantinga's work on the freewill defense, e.g., p. 254 n. 12. The use of "absolute" here is ambiguous. It is also important; on some definitions, his denial of "absolute power to contrary" could be reconciled with (some versions of) libertarianism. At any rate, I take him to be rejecting the principle of alternative possibilities. Further, he criticizes those scholastic uses of the notion of secondary causality (that insist that no sin is to be charged to God) on the grounds that they are "quasi-deistic and utterly foreign to the biblical material," p. 210. Moreover, he makes it clear that he wants to avoid the use of the term *concurrence* because it is "sometimes freighted with synergistic overtones," p. 210. Despite his concerns, however, he also admits that the "concept of second causes cannot simply be abandoned," p. 210.

[102]E.g., Robert A. Peterson and Michael D. Williams, *Why I Am Not an Arminian* (Downers Grove, IL: IVP Academic, 2004), pp. 137, 149.

[103]E.g., Douglas Groothuis, *Christian Apologetics: A Comprehensive Case for Biblical Faith* (Downers Grove, IL: IVP Academic, 2011), p. 636.

[104]Carson, *Difficult Doctrine*, p. 52.

[105]Carson, *Divine Sovereignty*, p. 10.

the brothers who sold Joseph into slavery. I am confident that all parties would read the narrative as displaying this much; the brothers conspire, and clearly they "intend it for evil." As Carson himself notes, "The text will not allow the brothers to be classed as puppets and thus to escape their guilt."[106] So it *is* wicked human machination. Carson denies that it is wicked human action into which God "intervened" to bring forth good. So is the problem with the language of intervention? Well, there may not be miraculous divine intervention here, but there is providential divine action throughout the story. Indeed, I am confident that this is what Carson is intending to safeguard. I would agree with him that divine providence is on display in this narrative, but he does not show that we need compatibilism to make such an affirmation. Perhaps he is exercised to combat the notion that God merely learns of the wicked human machination and reacts to it. Maybe the *"post eventu"* is really key here—maybe Carson's real concern is to counter the claims of "open theists" and others that God had no definite foresight or plan but was only reacting "on the fly." But such protestations would not be relevant to those who don't subscribe to open theism (and their kin), and at any rate we are left to conclude that he gives us no reason to think that compatibilism is the only—or even the best—explanation of this text.

Consider again Carson's claims about what he refers to as "perhaps the most striking instance of compatibilism" (Acts 4:23-31). Carson is sure that it would be wrong-headed to see the crucifixion of Christ—the turning point of all human history—"solely in terms of the conspiracy of the political authorities at the time, and *not* in terms of God's plan."[107] I agree with Carson that it would be a mistake to ignore or downplay the element of divine plan here. But it is hard to see how this could be taken as an argument for the divine determinism of all things (or even of this event). So far as I can see, it could function as an argument for soft determinism only if we assume that the only and exclusive options are these: an event must be either determined or unplanned. But since Carson offers us no reason to think that this event must have been either determined or unplanned, there is no reason to think that the argument

---

[106]Ibid.
[107]Carson, *Difficult Doctrine*, p. 53.

from biblical theology amounts to anything like a slam-dunk case for compatibilism. In other words, it gets us nowhere close to RA1 or RA2; neither can I see how it gets us to RA3. At most we are left with RA4. On the other hand, if there are alternative ways of accounting for a divine plan that are consistent with indeterminism, then this argument loses even more of its cogency. For instance, both Molinism and traditional Thomism offer different ways of understanding that Jesus Christ was "delivered up according to the definite plan and foreknowledge of God" (Acts 2:23), both of which are consistent with indeterminism and libertarian freedom.[108]

So far as I can see, we are a very long way from the conclusion that compatibilism is demanded by biblical theology, and we only get the impression that it is by using the same terms differently and talking past one another across the disciplines. For once we get clear on what compatibilism really is and isn't (as commonly understood to mean that freedom and/or responsibility are compatible with determinism), and then take a close look at the claims of biblical theology, it is not hard to see that these texts do not either affirm or entail the metaphysical thesis that, given the relevant natural laws and the history of this world (including, for the theist, all divine action), only one future could obtain. It seems safe to conclude (at least from these arguments from Carson) that the most that can be reasonably claimed for compatibilism is that compatibilism is consistent with the witness of the biblical narrative.

On the basis of the arguments surveyed, I judge this to be the *most* that can be claimed. But even this may be somewhat hasty. We might ask further: is compatibilism even consistent with biblical theology? This question becomes more interesting, and much more difficult, if we broaden our textual basis a bit and then relate that to the varied and competing versions of compatibilism. For while the biblical narrative indeed *is* concerned with moral responsibility—after all, the whole notion of sin is absolutely crucial to the canonical story, and this story makes no sense without it—it also showcases what strongly appears to be a concern for genuine freedom. Indeed, it ties moral responsibility to

---

[108]E.g., Thomas P. Flint, *Divine Providence: The Molinist Account* (Ithaca, NY: Cornell University Press, 1998); and Stump, *Aquinas*, pp. 455-78.

the choices that appear to be genuinely open to human agents. Consider the vast range of texts that are difficult to comprehend without a strong sense of conditionality.[109] In the canonical narrative, we see conditionality in Eden (Gen 2:16-17). Immediately out of Eden, Cain is told that he will be accepted if he does what is right—and then he is warned that if he does "not do what is right, sin is crouching" in wait for him (Gen 4:7). In the formation of Israel, God's declares his sovereignty and his election of Israel: "Although [or "because"] the whole earth is mine, you will be for me a kingdom of priests and a holy nation" (Ex 19:5-6). But included here as well is an unmistakable statement of contingency and conditionality: "if you obey me fully and keep my covenant" (Ex 19:5). The Torah is replete with conditional promises and warnings: "if you follow my decrees and are careful to obey my commands," "but if you will not listen to me and carry out all these commands, and if you reject my reject my decrees and abhor my laws and fail to carry out my commands and so violate my covenant," and so on (see, e.g., Lev 26:3-46; Deut 28:1-68). The choices are both real and stark: "See, I am setting before you today a blessing and a curse—the blessing if you obey the commands of the LORD your God . . . [and] the curse if you disobey the commands of the LORD your God" (Deut 11:26-28). Moses promises that Yahweh will "delight" in those who keep covenant faithfulness and obey God while they "turn to the LORD your God with all your heart and with all your soul" (Deut 30:9-10). He sets before them "life and death, blessings and curses," and he implores them to "choose life, so that you and your children may live and that you may love the LORD your God, listen to his voice, and hold fast to him" (Deut 30:19-20). Joshua echoes the main themes of this message from Moses (Josh 24:14-22).

Israel's history is filled with tales of the sad truth that it often did not choose obedience, covenant faithfulness and life. But its story is, nonetheless, indeed filled with opportunity for various choices. The word of God comes to David and instructs him to choose among three options (2 Sam 24:12). David recites the words of warning and promise to

---

[109]There are, of course, other sets of biblical texts and other theological concerns that are also challenging to square with compatibilism. The soteriological problem of evil looms especially large for any determinist who is not also a universalist.

Solomon (1 Kings 2:2-4), and Solomon echoes the same message at the dedication of the temple (1 Kings 8:25). Moreover, Yahweh appears to Solomon and repeats the promise of blessing and accompanying warning (1 Kings 9:4-9; cf. 1 Kings 11:11 and 2 Chron 7:11-22). As Israel and its leaders rebel against God, the promised judgment falls on them (e.g., 2 Kings 17:1-23), and the text makes it plain that their troubles came because they "had not obeyed the LORD their God, but had violated his covenant" (2 Kings 18:12). The Chronicler tells us that God's Spirit nonetheless offered opportunity for repentance and faithfulness: "The LORD is with you when you are with him. If you seek him, he will be found by you, but if you forsake him, he will forsake you" (2 Chron 15:2). Finally, their sin results in their conquest and exile. Upon return from exile, Ezra leaves no doubt as to its cause: it is their faithlessness and disobedience (e.g., Ezra 9:10-15). Nehemiah agrees (Neh 9:29-35). Israel's liturgists echo the same themes (e.g., Ps 78:31-64). Throughout this time, Israel's prophets offer hope—but only on conditions of repentance, faithfulness and obedience (e.g., Is 1:18-20; Jer 18:8; 26:1-6, 12-15; 35:12-17; Ezek 18:21-32; 33:10-16; Amos 5:4-6, 14-15; Zech 1:2-4). They also warn of impending disaster—but again this is predicated on willful rebellion (e.g., Is 8:6-8; 28:11-3; 30:1-5, 9-18; Jer 7:21-28; 11:1-8; Jer 18:9-12; 21:8-10; 22:4-9; 25:1-11). Isaiah reports the words of the Lord:

> I revealed myself to those who did not ask for me;
> I was found by those who did not seek me.
>
> To a nation that did not call on my name,
> I said, "Here am I, here am I."
>
> All day long I have held out my hands
> to an obstinate people. (Is 65:1-2; cf. Jer 7:13-15)

All this despite the fact that they repeatedly chose to do "what displeases" Yahweh (Is 66:4).

When we turn to the New Testament, we find accounts of those who are invited to be part of God's people but who "refused to come" (e.g., Mt 22:3). Jesus laments those who "refuse to come to me to have life" (Jn 5:40), and he laments in anguish over the awful reality that some of those whom he loves refuse to accept the salvation he offers: "Jerusalem, Jerusalem, you who kill the prophets and stone those sent to you, how often I have longed to gather your children together, as a hen gathers her chicks under her wings, and you were not willing" (Lk 13:34). Taken in a straightforward sense, this passage illustrates God's response to those who resist his will—it shows the incarnate Son's profound sorrow, for he "longs" to "gather," nurture and protect the very people who are "not willing" to come to him. The earliest apostolic preaching echoes this message as well: Stephen rehearses Israel's history and concludes that they "always resist the Holy Spirit" (Acts 7:51). Similarly, Paul is concerned that the Corinthians might "receive God's grace in vain" (2 Cor 6:1; cf. 2 Thess 1:5-10). Along similar lines, the author of Hebrews issues warnings that presuppose conditionality (e.g., Heb 3:7-19; 12:25) and make no sense without it.

What might we learn from this brief sketch? Of course compatibilists are well aware of such texts. As Carson says, such promises, challenges, invitations and commands "have bite precisely because they can be obeyed or disobeyed."[110] But how can compatibilists account for them? What does this mean for our consideration of compatibilism? Taken together, the message of these sorts of texts is not, I think, particularly good news for compatibilism. All compatibilists can note that, on their views as well as on libertarian accounts, agents indeed do deliberate and choose. So they have no problem affirming choice. Beyond this, note Carson's recognition that these exhortations, commands and warnings "have bite precisely because they can be obeyed or disobeyed." The sense of "can" (or "could have") here is, of course, crucial. But however we take it, things don't look all that great for the Frankfurt family of compatibilists (and semi-compatibilists). Such theorists typically deny that freedom and responsibility require the ability to do otherwise, but this overarching message of biblical theology seems to be saying that rebellious and unfaithful sinners sometimes are held responsible precisely because they don't (or didn't) do otherwise. As an example, consider 1 Corinthians 10:12-13: "So, if you think you are standing firm, be careful that you don't fall! No temptation has seized you except what is common

---

[110]Carson, *How Long*, p. 181.

to mankind. And God is faithful; he will not let you be tempted beyond what you can bear. But when you are tempted, he will also provide a way out so that you can endure it." As William Lane Craig points out, "It follows that any Christian who does not in some circumstance endure but succumbs to temptation had it within his power to take the way of escape instead, i.e., he had the liberty of opposites in those circumstances."[111] Here "God has provided a way of escape that one could have taken but that one has failed to do so. In other words, in precisely that situation, one had the power either to succumb or to take the way out—that is to say, one had libertarian freedom. It is precisely because one failed to take the divinely appointed way of escape that one is held accountable."[112] So while the Frankfurters deny that the ability to do otherwise is relevant for freedom and responsibility, in Scripture—at least sometimes—sinners are held responsible precisely for not having done otherwise.[113]

On the other hand, classical compatibilists often appeal to the "conditional" sense of "can" (along with other senses), thus allowing the compatibilist to say that the agent can do (or could have done) otherwise *in some sense(s)*. On this account, so long as the determining conditions—whatever combination of determining factors is decisive (for the relevant version of determinism)—had been different, then the outcome would have been different. As we have seen, critics of classical compatibilism point out that the conditional analysis only works so long as it keeps us focused on singular actions rather than on the big picture or the character of the agent. For this doctrine only allows us to say that we "could do" or "could have done" otherwise only until we probe further or dig deeper; as Taylor says, we always find that "we must retract and replace it with 'could not have been otherwise' as soon as we discover, as we must at each step, that whatever would have to have been different could not have been different."[114]

---

[111]William Lane Craig, "Ducking Friendly Fire: Davison on the Grounding Objection," *Philosophia Christi* 8 (2006): 163 n. 4.

[112]William Lane Craig, "A Middle Knowledge Response," in *Divine Foreknowledge: Four Views*, ed. James K. Beilby and Paul R. Eddy (Downers Grove, IL: InterVarsity Press, 2001), p. 202.

[113]Care should be taken here not to overconclude. I do not take the canonical account to imply (or even to suggest) that we are *always* able to do otherwise.

[114]Taylor, *Metaphysics*, p. 49.

Despite the common worries (held by fellow compatibilists as well as by incompatibilists), perhaps the classical compatibilist is better off than her Frankfurt cousins. Perhaps. The critics of classical compatibilism worry that what "can do otherwise" really means is only that the agent can do otherwise only if whatever would have to have been different had been different—and thus doesn't do nearly enough to help the compatibilist. They worry that "can do otherwise" really means nothing more than that an agent could have acted differently only if the relevant determining factors were different. But when Moses sets "blessings and curses" before Israel, he warns them not to say that they cannot really do what he challenges them to do: "now what I am commanding you today is not too difficult for you or beyond your reach" (Deut 30:11). He isn't suggesting that they have anything like merely conditional ability to choose differently; he surely isn't saying that they could choose rightly if only the conditions were different. Plausibly, he doesn't merely mean that this wouldn't be too difficult for them *if things were different*; apparently, he means that this *isn't* too difficult for them or beyond their reach. Indeed, *that* is why they have no excuse. Returning to 1 Corinthians 10:13, the situation seems similar. As Anthony Thiselton puts it, in making a way of escape "God provides, marks, and renders the believer *able* (δύνασθαι) to use" it.[115] If the believer is currently able to use the way of escape, then it is not plausible to interpret Paul as saying that the way of escape would offer hope if only the past (or the laws of nature or logic) were different. Paul is writing to encourage believers about what in fact *is* the case—they have a way of escape open to them. Moreover, the classical compatibilist—along with her Frankfurt family—still faces the deep concerns about moral responsibility. So while the classical compatibilist may be somewhat better off than her Frankfurt cousins with respect to biblical theology, it is far from obvious that she is out of the woods.

Concluding observations. I do not intend this discussion to be taken as a refutation of compatibilism. I know that it is not. Even less is it a demonstration of libertarianism (the conjunction of the thesis that some agents are free and the thesis that freedom is incompatible with

---

[115]Anthony C. Thiselton, *The First Epistle to the Corinthians: A Commentary on the Greek Text* (Grand Rapids: Eerdmans, 2000), p. 749.

determinism).[116] The issues are far-reaching and complicated, and much more would need to be done to accomplish either task. The libertarian cannot simply point to a set of scriptural texts that portray human decision-making and choice and claim victory over compatibilists. At the same time, neither can the compatibilist simply point to a select set of biblical texts and claim a biblical proof of compatibilism. Lack of quick and easy victory for either side does not, however, mean that either biblical theology or metaphysical considerations are useless in these discussions. To the contrary, any genuine progress in these discussions will need expertise in both fields. For while the analytic arguments can be extremely helpful in making the necessary judgments, they do not provide the kind of theological insight that is provided by biblical theology. And while the biblical account is vital to any adequate theology of divine providence (and accompanying doctrines of human responsibility, sin and grace), the canonical narrative does not itself give us the kind of analytic tools that are needed to make progress. We may conclude that it presupposes the proper use of such tools, but it does not make them explicit. Biblical theology can give us the important theological desiderata, and theological analysis can help us both understand and formulate the doctrinal conclusions. This does not mean that analytic theology finally supersedes or replaces biblical theology; nothing here implies that biblical theology is merely some pile of theological data or confused, immature rendering that only provides some raw materials for analytic theology and then can safely be discarded once the "real" work of analytic theology has been done. To the contrary, one may affirm what I have said to this point and also affirm the continuing importance of a biblical theology that follows the shape of the canonical narrative. In other words, analytic theology may be a complement to biblical theology; it need not replace or undermine biblical theology.

Using this discussion as a kind of case study of the relationship between analytic theology and biblical theology, I hope to have clarified a few points. First, in this case, the work of biblical theologians such as Carson is important and can be very helpful. It is common—and maybe

---

[116]Cf. Rea, *Metaphysics*, p. 210.

far too easy—for analytically oriented discussions of issues related to divine foreknowledge and sovereignty and human freedom and responsibility to be heavily (or even sometimes exclusively) metaphysical. In such contexts, the work of biblical theologians such as Carson can be immensely helpful in various ways: such work can help to contextualize or locate the metaphysical and doctrinal debates in their proper place in the flow of the biblical narrative, and such work can be vital in reminding analytic theologians of the crucial biblical desiderata and in holding them accountable to it. In particular, I judge Carson to have done us a major service in this respect. He is right, I am convinced, to remind us that neither divine sovereignty nor moral responsibility is negotiable. Moreover, he is helpful in pointing out various important elements of the biblical portrayal of divine sovereignty. His work can help us gain a clearer, sharper vision of the parameters of any theologically acceptable account of divine and human action, and it can help us see how this account fits into the "narrative coherence" of Scripture.

But it is also common—and probably far too easy—for discussions of the same issues that are attentive to exegetical concerns and grounded in biblical theology to proceed without sufficient carefulness. Here is where the analytic theologian can be of great help. For while the biblical theologian can help us with the "narrative coherence," the analytic theologian can assist with logical coherence. In this case, it should be clear that analysis reveals that what Carson calls "compatibilism" really isn't compatibilism. (Of course anyone is free to use whatever term they desire, but one should do so with a clear awareness that their usage is importantly different.) Accordingly, his arguments for "compatibilism" simply do not succeed as exegetical or biblical-theological support for compatibilism. To the contrary, his work might help us eliminate at least some versions of compatibilism. Indeed, William Lane Craig and J. P. Moreland conclude that Carson's work actually works to undermine compatibilism, for it helps us see that "a deterministic understanding of divine providence" is ruled out by the very passages adduced by Carson.[117] Analytic theology can also help in moving the discussion forward; it can

---

[117]Moreland and Craig, *Philosophical Foundations*, p. 561.

clarify where future arguments need to be forthcoming, where there is agreement, where the "fault lines" lie in the discussion, how various arguments might work to support either compatibilism or incompatibilism (and either determinism or indeterminism), and how cumulative case arguments might work for either side.

3

Analytic Theology and the History of Doctrine

Serious theological work is forced, again and again, to begin from
the beginning. However, as this is done, the theology of past periods,
classical and less classical, also plays a part and demands a hearing. . . .
Augustine, Thomas Aquinas, Luther, Schleiermacher and all the
rest are not dead but living. They still speak, and
demand a hearing as living voices.

KARL BARTH

A NALYTIC THEOLOGY, as *theology*, should be done in response to divine revelation. For Christians who take Holy Scripture as that revelation or as an accurate and reliable reflection of it, engagement with exegesis and biblical theology is an essential part of the theological task. But we are not, of course, the first readers of Scripture, and we stand to benefit from the history of interpretation and the development of Christian doctrine. This raises further questions about analytic theology and its relation to the Christian tradition and to the discipline of historical theology. In this chapter, I first look at the relation of analytic theology to historical theology and to what is sometimes called "retrieval

Epigraph: Karl Barth, *Protestant Theology in the Nineteenth Century*, new ed. (Grand Rapids: Eerdmans, 2002), p. 3.

theology." Following this, I offer two case studies. Both are in Christology. One shows how analytic theology can help us to better understand and defend classical orthodoxy in light of contemporary objections to it; the other shows how the creedal orthodoxy might serve as a guide to recent constructive work in analytic theology.

HISTORICAL THEOLOGY AND ANALYTIC THEOLOGY

Analytic theology as historical theology. Some of the current literature in analytic theology shows evidence of very significant overlap with historical theology. Indeed, it is safe to say that some of it really just *is* historical theology. Analytic theology is sometimes criticized, as we saw in the first chapter, for being insensitive to the development of doctrine. Sometimes these criticisms are warranted. Analytic theologians may be quick to isolate a particular text and try to break it down to find the real "core" of the doctrine, or they may find the historical context of little relevance to the sober truth. Indeed, analytic theologians sometimes seem to "think of ancient texts as cumbersome delivery systems containing ideas which it is their job to extract from the delivery system and do something with."[1]

Sometimes the criticisms are warranted—but not always! For some analytic theologians are at the forefront of careful, contextual historical research. Richard Cross, Jeffrey Brower, Scott MacDonald, Marilyn McCord Adams, Norman Kretzmann, Eleonore Stump, Timothy Pawl and many others stand out for their exemplary and exacting historical scholarship. To use important analytic treatments of the doctrine of the Trinity as an example, and to focus even further on later medieval theology, we can see considerable contributions. Richard Cross has offered significant insight into the theology of John Duns Scotus (in particular);[2] Paul Thom has surveyed and analyzed the metaphysics of the Trinity from Augustine through Boethius, Abelard, Gilbert of Poitiers, Peter Lombard, Bonaventure, Albert the Great, Thomas Aquinas and Duns

---

[1]Fred Sanders, "The State of the Doctrine of the Trinity in Evangelical Theology," *Southwestern Journal of Theology* 47 (2005): 169.
[2]E.g., Richard Cross, *Duns Scotus on God* (Aldershot, UK: Ashgate, 2005), pp. 127-248.

Scotus to William of Ockham;[3] Russell L. Friedman has undertaken a similar task;[4] Jeffrey E. Brower has examined Abelard's use of the analogy of material constitution;[5] J. T. Paasch has provided us with a focused look at the doctrines of generation and procession in the theologies of Henry of Ghent, Duns Scotus and William of Ockham;[6] and Scott Williams has given us a study of the variety in late medieval trinitarian theology.[7] This is work in analytic theology that really is primarily an exercise in historical theology; these scholars are studying the history of doctrine with the "style and ambitions" of analytic theology (and are using the tools of the analytic tradition) to help understand and explicate medieval trinitarian theology. Much the same could be said about other issues and loci; theological anthropology, hamartiology, the divine attributes, Christology, eschatology and many more areas are being probed as well.

Analytic theology as retrieval theology. Other analytic theology listens closely and respectfully to the tradition but seeks to go beyond exposition and explanation. This work actively evaluates various theological proposals from the tradition, and does so critically as it tries to mine the riches of the tradition for theological materials that will be useful in constructive work. Sometimes called "retrieval theology," this is what John Webster calls a *"mode* of theology" rather than a distinct method or school of thought.[8] As Webster describes it, retrieval theology resists the notion that the history of modern theology is "simply one of the defenselessness of Christian self-description against the onslaught of critical reason"; instead it sees "the failure to marshal specifi-

---

[3]Paul Thom, *The Logic of the Trinity: Augustine to Ockham* (New York: Fordham University Press, 2012).

[4]E.g., Russell L. Friedman, *Medieval Trinitarian Thought from Aquinas to Ockham* (Cambridge: Cambridge University Press, 2010).

[5]E.g., Jeffrey E. Brower, "Abelard on the Trinity," in *The Cambridge Companion to Abelard*, ed. Jeffrey E. Brower and K. Guilfoy (Cambridge: Cambridge University Press, 2004), pp. 233-57.

[6]J. T. Paasch, *Divine Production in Late Medieval Trinitarian Theology: Henry of Ghent, Duns Scotus, and William Ockham* (Oxford: Oxford University Press, 2012).

[7]Scott Williams, "Indexicals and the Trinity: Two Non-Social Models," *Journal of Analytic Theology* 1 (2013): 74-94.

[8]John Webster, "Theologies of Retrieval," in *The Oxford Handbook of Systematic Theology*, ed. John Webster, Kathryn Tanner and Iain Torrance (Oxford: Oxford University Press, 2007), p. 584.

cally theological resources to meet its detractors."[9] It thus treats "premodern Christian theology as a resource rather than problem."[10] Historical work is, of course, very important here, for it "enables theologies of retrieval to place, interpret, and in some measure transcend the constraints of modern theology by unearthing the neglect and disorder by which they are imposed," and it allows for "the reclamation of tracts of the Christian past as a resource for present constructive work."[11] Put baldly, one must really know the past—and not just a shadowy simulacrum of our own preferred position that we call "the tradition"—in order to reclaim it. So solid, careful historical work is vital to retrieval theology.

But if retrieval theology presupposes and relies on historical theology, it also goes beyond it. It receives these resources realistically, recognizing the historical location and limitations of various views. And it receives these resources gratefully, looking for potential for "furthering the theological task."[12] But it also receives them critically, with a commitment to careful evaluation and analysis of them. As such, analytic theology is a natural ally of retrieval theology. And while neither Webster nor the current analytic practitioners call attention to the connection, in point of fact this is what many analytic theologians are actually doing.

To stay once again with the doctrine of the Trinity as an example, Brian Leftow has articulated and defended what he calls "Latin trinitarianism."[13] He does not refer to it as, say, "Anselmian" or "Thomist" or "Scotist" trinitarianism, and there is very good reason for him to refrain from doing so. For his work on the doctrine of the Trinity *isn't* Anselmian, or Thomist, or Scotist. It does not first articulate and then try to defend their views (either collectively or distributively). It is "Latin" trinitarianism in this broad sense: Leftow adopts what he sees as important theological desiderata delivered by the mainstream Latin tradition, and he takes some cues from these theologians with respect to formulation. In other words, he accepts what he takes to be central to the

---

[9]Ibid., p. 586.
[10]Ibid., p. 585.
[11]Ibid., pp. 589-90.
[12]Ibid., p. 596.
[13]E.g., Brian Leftow, "A Latin Trinity," *Faith and Philosophy* (2004): 304-33.

Latin tradition in general, and defends this by a strategy that is creative and even novel in many respects. Whether or not he is finally successful is another matter (I have my doubts about several aspects of it);[14] it is his approach and aims that are important here. He is doing retrieval theology in the sense that he is both (1) receiving and appropriating important theological claims and insights of the medieval Latin tradition, and (2) defending these claims and pressing them into the service of constructive theology in creative ways.

The work of William Hasker is methodologically similar in many respects. Although his own theological proposals are very different from those of Leftow, he is also doing what may be called retrieval theology. He looks to the theology of the major fourth-century theologians (including both the Cappadocians and Augustine), and he relies on important work done by patrologists who specialize in the study of the trinitarian theology of the fourth and fifth centuries.[15] He then critically receives, defends and develops important elements of that theology in defense of a moderate "social trinitarianism."[16]

Leftow and Hasker provide us with examples of retrieval theology that are fairly "loose"; others will be "tighter" in the sense that they try to stay closer to the details of the tradition.[17] Beyond the doctrine of the Trinity, the situation is similar with respect to other issues and loci: theological anthropology, hamartiology, theology proper (divine attributes), Christology, eschatology and others are sites of ongoing work in analytic theology in the mode of "retrieval."

Analytic theology and Christian orthodoxy. For Christians who take

---

[14]E.g., Thomas H. McCall, *Which Trinity? Whose Monotheism? Systematic and Philosophical Theologians on the Metaphysics of Trinitarian Theology* (Grand Rapids: Eerdmans, 2010), pp. 112-22; Michael C. Rea, "The Trinity," in *Oxford Handbook of Philosophical Theology*, ed. Thomas P. Flint and Michael C. Rea (Oxford: Oxford University Press, 2009), pp. 700-704; William Hasker, "A Leftovian Trinity?," *Faith and Philosophy* (2009): 154-66.

[15]See especially Lewis Ayres, *Nicaea and Its Legacy: An Approach to Fourth-Century Trinitarian Theology* (Oxford: Oxford University Press, 2004); Ayres, *Augustine and the Trinity* (Cambridge: Cambridge University Press, 2010); Khaled Anatolios, *Retrieving Nicaea: The Development and Meaning of Trinitarian Doctrine* (Grand Rapids: Baker Academic, 2011).

[16]William Hasker, *Metaphysics and the Tri-Personal God* (Oxford: Oxford University Press, 2013).

[17]I attempt to do this in "Trinity Doctrine, Plain and Simple," in *Advancing Trinitarian Theology: Explorations in Constructive Dogmatics*, ed. Oliver D. Crisp and Fred Sanders (Grand Rapids: Zondervan Academic, 2014), pp. 42-59.

Scripture to be divine revelation (or an accurate and reliable reflection or record of that revelation), it is supremely authoritative in theology.[18] It is, then, the "norming norm" (*norma normans*) that is authoritative above any and all other sources of theological authority and is thus able to guide, challenge and correct us. Oliver Crisp says it this way: the Bible is the "final arbiter of matters theological for Christians as the particular place in which God reveals himself to his people"; it is the "first order authority in all matters of Christian doctrine."[19]

But Scripture is never interpreted in a vacuum. We stand in a long line of witnesses to this divine revelation, and we can receive that witnessing tradition gratefully. We can, then, look at it as a resource rather than an obstacle. In other words, there is every reason for constructive analytic theology to work in the mode of retrieval. But there is no such thing as "*the* tradition" (understood as a monolithic and uniform body of teaching), and it is important to distinguish between various types of engagement with elements of the tradition of Christian doctrinal development.

At one level, creedal orthodoxy should serve as a doctrinal authority; the ecumenical creeds are the "norm" that is "normed by" (*norma normata*) Holy Scripture but then that serve to shape and correct subsequent theological work. This creedal tradition has the deepest and broadest authority within Christian theology, and all Christians who accept these creeds (as making "realist" claims in some sense) will seek to develop constructive theological proposals that are consistent with, and guided by, these ecumenical creeds. Beyond these creeds, however, there are also the theological confessions of particular ecclesial traditions and bodies. These often go far beyond the ecumenical creeds in both scope and detail; they also, often by this very extended scope and detail, preclude many potential developments and exclude the beliefs and confessions of other traditions. If we accept the confessions of particular ecclesial bodies as a third tier of authority (standing under

---

[18]I argue that there is an important sense in which Scripture should be taken *as* revelation in my "On Understanding Scripture as the Word of God," in *Analytic Theology: New Essays in the Philosophy of Theology*, ed. Oliver D. Crisp and Michael C. Rea (Oxford: Oxford University Press, 2009), pp. 171-86.

[19]Oliver D. Crisp, *God Incarnate: Explorations in Christology* (New York: T & T Clark, 2009), p. 17.

the creeds and ultimately under Scripture as it bears witness to God's revelation that culminates in Christ), then we will look to them as important and helpful guides.

This means, of course, that those theologians who *belong* to those distinct traditions will receive them gratefully and take them seriously: to draw on some ready examples, traditional Lutheran theologians will submit to the Augsburg Confession, the Formula of Concord and other important confessions; traditional Reformed theologians will accept the teachings of the Westminster Confession of Faith, the Belgic Confession, the Canons of Dordt and other key statements; faithful Anglicans will hold to the Thirty-Nine Articles of Religion; and, of course, Roman Catholic theologians will accept the body of official magisterial teaching. And so on. They will do so with varying levels of agreement about some of those confessional statements, and they will do so with variant understandings of "subscriptionism" ("strict" or "loose"). But to the extent that they are, say, *Lutheran* or *Reformed* theologians in any recognizably traditional sense of those terms, they will receive their confessions as reliable (if fallible and corrigible) authorities. This much may seem obvious, but I suggest that for the sake of constructive analytic theology moving forward, it is helpful for theologians to also know and respectfully engage other confessional traditions. Unless the theologian has good reason to conclude that there is nothing to gain from such an exercise, careful and humble engagement with the theology of other confessional traditions may be mutually beneficial.

Beyond these formal statements (creeds and confessions), the work of the prominent theologians of the church catholic deserves our deep respect and can be a great resource in constructive analytic theology. Again, it seems important for theologians to know the major theologians of their own traditions. Thus Lutherans will be acquainted with, and respectful of, the work of not only Martin Luther and Philipp Melanchthon but also Martin Chemnitz, Johann Wilhelm Baier, Johann Andreas Quenstadt, Johann Gerhard and many others. Reformed theologians will appreciate not only the work of John Calvin but also the efforts of such luminaries as Peter Martyr Vermigli, Martin Bucer, Theodore Beza, Franciscus Junius and John Owen, as well as a great host of lesser-known figures. Roman Catholics will, naturally enough, be engaged with the work of such massive legacies as those of Francisco Suarez, Louis de Molina and many more. And so on. There are scores of important theologians from each of the major traditions—many of them largely forgotten—whose work awaits further exploration. But contemporary theologians from all these traditions (and others) may also access the thought of important patristic and medieval theologians—they share an important common tradition. And, of course, they may profit from engagement with the major theologians of these other confessional traditions as well.

In doing so, it is important for the analytic theologian to listen carefully to the work of scholars who specialize in historical theology. The work of constructive analytic theology should not be confused with that of historical theology; neither should it be reduced to it. The constructive analytic theologian who wishes to benefit from the tradition—to benefit from its advances as well as to learn from its mistakes—will seek to go beyond repetition and description. But if the work of the analytic theologian should not be reduced to historical theology, neither is the analytic theologian free simply to troll through the ocean of the history of doctrine hoping to hook some juicy quotations, pull them out of context and then press them into service. Instead, it seems to me that it is much better for the theologian to engage the relevant texts themselves (in translation, where possible, but also in the original languages where this is helpful) and the important work of the historical specialists.[20]

If Christian tradition functions as authoritative (as the *norma normata* that is subordinate to the *norma normans* that is Holy Scripture), then what does it mean to say that some theological proposal is "orthodox" or "classical"? How is some proffered theological proposition *P* really "authorized" by the traditional or "classical" orthodoxy? Once we get clear on what the relevant sense of "tradition" in view really is, we will be in a position to consider the differences between some theological claim being *demanded by classical/confessional orthodoxy, con-*

---

[20]This echoes my comments in Thomas H. McCall, "Relational Trinity: Creedal Perspective," in *Two Views on the Doctrine of the Trinity*, ed. Jason S. Sexton (Grand Rapids: Zondervan Academic, 2014), pp. 114-15.

sistent with classical/confessional orthodoxy or *inconsistent with classical/ confessional orthodoxy.*[21]

Two cases studies may serve to demonstrate how the Christian tradition (informed by historical theology) might interface with analytic theology. In the first, analytic theology is informed by both current work in metaphysics and the history of doctrine as it engages with some important criticisms of the classical Christian doctrine of the incarnation. Here we see analytic theologians actively doing retrieval theology to help us understand and defend classical Christian orthodoxy. In the second, we see analytic theology that draws on classical orthodoxy to interact critically with a recent proposal in analytic philosophy of religion.

OBJECTIONS, ONTOLOGY AND ORTHODOXY: CHRISTOLOGY AS A CASE STUDY

The central Christian doctrine. Orthodox Christians believe that Jesus Christ is a person who is both human and divine. Existing as one person, he nonetheless possesses two "natures." In the words of the Chalcedonian Formula (451), he possesses these natures "without confusion, without change, without division, without separation; the distinction in natures being in no way annulled by the union." For centuries, and all over the world, such belief has been bedrock for Christian orthodoxy.

Yet for all the width and depth of Christian commitment to classical orthodoxy, criticisms have beset the doctrine. Famously, John Hick has claimed that "to say, without further explanation, that the historical Jesus of Nazareth was also God is as devoid of meaning as to say that this circle drawn with a pencil on paper is also a square."[22]

Orthodoxy, objections and the mind(s) of Christ. Faced with such

---

[21]Getting clear on this is beyond the scope of this essay; I am here raising formal rather than material considerations. But, plausibly, for all Christians committed to classical orthodoxy, it includes adherence to the major christological and trinitarian creeds. Roman Catholic theologians will follow their own magisterial teaching, various Protestant traditions will take their own confessions seriously, etc.

[22]John Hick, "Jesus and the World Religions," in *The Myth of God Incarnate*, ed. John Hick (London: SCM Press, 1977), p. 178. Hick appears to have backed off of his earlier claims about logical incoherence, but even his later work insists that it is not possible to have a view that is coherent while also orthodox and religiously meaningful, e.g., John Hick, *The Metaphor of God Incarnate: Christology in a Pluralistic Age* (Louisville: Westminster John Knox, 1993), pp. 4, 58-59.

criticisms, proponents of the orthodox doctrine have responded in a variety of ways. Drawing on different metaphysical resources, and sometimes weighing the desiderata of orthodox Christology somewhat differently, they have proposed various defenses of the doctrine. Even a brief survey of this literature shows that there are many options for responding to charges such as those of Hick.

Thomas V. Morris's important work *The Logic of God Incarnate* articulates and defends an abstractist account (where the natures are to be understood as properties rather than as specific, concrete and particular natures).[23] He draws several important distinctions: the distinction between an individual-essence and a kind-essence, the distinction between common and essential human properties, and the distinction between being fully human and being merely human. An individual-essence (or *hacceity*) is the set of properties that one must have to be *this* distinct individual. Put more precisely, a person's individual-essence is the full set of properties that is possessed by that person in all possible worlds in which that person exists.[24] Alvin Plantinga puts it like this: "An essence E of an object x is a property it has essentially which is furthermore such that it is not possible that there be something distinct from x that has E."[25] (Compare Graeme Forbes: "a set of properties I which satisfies the following two conditions: every property P in I is an essential property of I, and it is not possible that some object y distinct from x has every member of I.")[26] A kind-essence (or kind-nature), on the other hand, is what Morris describes as the full set of "properties individually necessary and jointly sufficient" for inclusion in that kind. They are individually necessary: you must have all of them to be a member of that kind. And "jointly sufficient" means that if you have all of them, then indeed you are

---

[23]See also Richard Swinburne, *The Christian God* (Oxford: Oxford University Press, 1994), pp. 192-215. For an abstractist account that offers a different view of the consciousness of Christ, see Joseph Jedwab, "The Incarnation and Unity of Consciousness," in *The Metaphysics of the Incarnation*, ed. Anna Marmadoro and Jonathan Hill (Oxford: Oxford University Press, 2011), pp. 168-85.

[24]For important background, see Alvin Plantinga, *The Nature of Necessity* (Oxford: Oxford University Press, 1974); and Kenneth Konyndyk, *Introductory Modal Logic* (Notre Dame, IN: University of Notre Dame Press, 1986).

[25]Alvin Plantinga, "Essence and Essentialism," in *A Companion of Metaphysics*, ed. Jaegwon Kim and Ernest Sosa (Oxford: Blackwell, 1995), p. 139.

[26]Graeme Forbes, *The Metaphysics of Modality* (Oxford: Oxford University Press, 1985), p. 99.

a member of that kind. So "human nature comprises all those properties individually necessary and jointly sufficient for being human," and no one can be divine without having all the properties individually necessary and jointly sufficient for being divine. "No individual can be human without having each and every one of the properties essential to humanity. And likewise for divinity. For example, on the traditional doctrine of God, properties essential for divinity include omnipresence, omniscience, aseity, eternality, and the like. No individual can be God without having all such properties."[27] Morris puts this distinction to work; at this point the important thing to see is that when we speak of "natures" or "essences" we need to take care to avoid a common confusion.

The second important distinction Morris draws is between *common* and *essential* human properties. Morris points out that this distinction is often missed by people who use the language of "nature" or "essence" to mean something like "what is characteristic of" something. But while this is a common, and indeed understandable, confusion, it is a damaging one nonetheless. An object "has a property essentially if and only if it has it and could not possibly have lacked it," if it has it in every possible world in which that object exists.[28] A common human property, as Morris lays it out, is any property that is possessed by many or most humans. Indeed, we could extend this to include all humans. But the fact that most (or perhaps even all) humans have a property does not entail that it is essential. Morris offers this illustration:

> The property of living at some time on the surface of the earth is a common human property. I think that is safe to assume that it is now a universal property for humans. But it is not an element of human nature. It is not essential for being human. It is clearly possible that at some time in the future human beings be born, live, and die on a space station or another planet colonized by earth, without ever setting foot on the earth itself. This is an obvious example of our distinction. The property of living at some time on the surface of the earth may now be a universal human property, but it is not an essential one.[29]

---

[27]Thomas V. Morris, *The Logic of God Incarnate* (Ithaca, NY: Cornell University Press, 1986), pp. 22-23.

[28]Plantinga, "Essence and Essentialism," p. 138.

[29]Morris, *Logic of God Incarnate*, p. 63.

So a common human property simply is one that is possessed by most (or even all) human persons, while an essential human property is a property that belongs to the kind-nature. While common human properties are *usually* possessed by human persons, essential human properties are those that *must* be possessed by humans.

This leads Morris to his third distinction: that between being *merely* human and being *fully* human. To be fully human is to exemplify the kind-essence of humanity, while to be merely human is to exemplify *only* that kind-essence. As Morris summarizes it, his point is that

> the kind-nature exemplified distinctively by all human beings is that of humanity. To be a human being is to exemplify human nature. An individual is fully human just in case he fully exemplifies human nature. To be merely human is not to exemplify a kind-nature, a natural kind, distinct from that of humanity; it is rather to exemplify humanity without also exemplifying any ontologically higher kind, such as divinity.[30]

Morris employs these distinctions to argue that Chalcedonian Christology should not be dismissed as incoherent. To the contrary, he finds it "logically above reproach."[31] While it is of course true that the property of being *merely* human is a common human property, this is no reason to suppose that it must be an essential property. And, after all, Christians readily affirm that the incarnation of the Son of God as Jesus of Nazareth was a unique occurrence. But this does not license us to think that the incarnation is impossible, for so long as we keep this crucial distinction in mind, claims such as those of Hick appear to be overstated and indeed indefensible. As Morris reminds us, the central Christian claim is not that incarnation is a usual occurrence; to the contrary, it is radically surprising. Nonetheless, however, being unusual or surprising should not be confused with being impossible. As Morris puts it, "The Chalcedonian claim is not that Jesus was merely human. It is rather that he was, and is, fully human in addition to being divine."[32]

So on Morris's account, the Logos is fully divine: the second person of the Holy Trinity has all the divine attributes. In the incarnation, the eternal

---

[30]Ibid., p. 66.
[31]Ibid., p. 46.
[32]Ibid., p. 66.

Logos also becomes fully and completely human as the Son takes on himself the full set of properties individually necessary and jointly sufficient for being a member of the kind-essence humanity. He does not cease to be divine when he becomes human; he is fully divine but after the incarnation not merely divine, and he is fully human (since the incarnation) but never merely human. He is fully divine and fully human, and he is so as one person: the Logos, the second person of the Holy Trinity.

Morris wields this careful metaphysical reasoning to turn back such charges as those made by Hick. He is, however, well aware of some remaining challenges.[33] Making such metaphysical and logical maneuvers is helpful to an extent, but it leaves unaddressed several key questions. How, for instance, is the incarnate Son both omniscient and nonomniscient? As divine, the Son is omniscient. As human, however, it would seem that he is nonomniscient. Morris cannot simply claim that nonomniscience is only a common (rather than essential) property of humanity, for he is well aware that Scripture also teaches that Jesus is nonomniscient. The Gospel accounts are too clear: Jesus grew in wisdom (Lk 2:52), and he plainly confesses ignorance (Mk 13:32). So we have an apparent contradiction after all: Jesus is omniscient (if divine), and Jesus is ignorant (according to the clear teaching of Scripture). How does Morris's model try to account for such a contradiction?

Morris offers a "two-minds" proposal. On this view, Jesus Christ has "something like two ranges of consciousness."[34] The divine Logos, the second person of the Holy Trinity, has the divine mind. It is, by virtue of being divine, not only very knowledgeable but also omniscient. In addition, in the incarnation the Son takes upon himself a human mind. It is, by virtue of being human, limited in knowledge and understanding. It is marked by its location in space and time; it was "thoroughly human, Jewish, and first-century Palestinian in nature."[35] Due to his divine mind,

---

[33]Philosophers of biology are commonly convinced that analysis of biological species does not work well in terms of necessary and sufficient conditions (instead preferring to think of biological species in terms of cluster concepts). So another potential worry (one that Morris does not deal with) is this: his proposal might be committed either to an implausible biological thesis or to the denial that human nature is a biological kind.

[34]Ibid., p. 102.

[35]Ibid., p. 103.

the Son is omniscient. Due to his human mind, the Son knows what a first-century Jewish man would know.

How are these two "minds" (or "ranges of consciousness") related? Perhaps more importantly, how might they be tightly enough related for their bearer to count as *one* person (as Christian orthodoxy insists)? Morris explains that they are related in this way: "The divine mind of God the Son contained, but was not contained by, his earthly mind, or range of consciousness."[36] He posits what he calls an "asymmetric accessing relation" between the divine mind and the human mind. The divine mind, as omniscient, has full and uninterrupted access to the contents of the human mind. The human mind, on the other hand, only has access to the contents of the divine mind on certain important occasions. So when we read in the Gospel accounts that Jesus foretells the future or sees into the hearts of his friends and enemies, we are to conclude that in these moments the divine mind "uploads" the pertinent (but otherwise inaccessible) information to the human mind. On the other hand, when we read in the Gospels that Jesus "grew in wisdom" (Lk 2:52) or professes ignorance (Mk 13:32), we are to understand this in a straightforward way. For the human mind of Jesus grew and developed roughly as human minds do, and on many occasions the divine mind does not "upload" the relevant information. On Morris's account, there is "a metaphysical and personal depth to the man Jesus [that is] lacking in the case of every individual who is merely human."[37] So Jesus is unique—but this much is Christian orthodoxy; Jesus Christ is fully human, but he is not merely human.

Morris is convinced that his view "allows for the apparent intellectual and spiritual growth of Jesus in his humanity to be a real development," and it also has the resources to "account for, or at least to allow for, the cry of dereliction."[38] He is sure that it avoids the heresies associated with Christology. Nonetheless, he is sensitive to worries that somehow this model compromises the "unity of the person" of Christ. "But can we

---

[36]Ibid.
[37]Ibid.
[38]Ibid.

really understand what it is to attribute two minds . . . to one person?"[39] Morris offers several analogies (which he readily admits are of only limited usefulness). He suggests that perhaps cases of brain-hemisphere commissurotomy, multiple personalities and even hypnosis can shed some light on how one person can be said to have multiple "ranges of consciousness." He insists "that as a matter of fact, in some cases of multiple personality, there exists one personality with apparently and direct knowledge of the experiences had, information gained, and actions initiated by one or more other personalities, a sort of knowledge which is not had by any other personality concerning it. In other words, there seem to be existing asymmetric accessing relations in such cases."[40]

Of course Morris is aware that such cases are usually referred to as multiple personality *disorders*, and he is quick to show that he does not intend such analogies to serve as a "complete modeling of the noetic features of the incarnation."[41] Nonetheless, he thinks that the analogies work to show at least the possibility of two minds in one person, and they go some distance toward raising the plausibility as well: "If one troubling aberrant personality is eliminated therapeutically from the behavioral repertoire of someone afflicted with multiple personalities, the therapist surely need not see the effect of her work as the killing of a person."[42]

Perhaps more promising is Morris's account of the dream phenomena reported by many people. Consider the case of someone who is dreaming deeply: a seminary student falls asleep while studying for a final exam in church history and has a full, HD-quality, high-octane, action-adventure dream. In her dream, she is being pursued through dark woods by hooded men on horseback. She stumbles on an inn lit by firelight, and there she is rescued by a big man carrying a sword. As she is spirited away with her rescuer, she learns that he is none other than Martin Luther. The dream is powerful and vivid, with a full range and depth of emotional experience. But then, at a moment of great peril, the realization that she is dreaming begins to dawn on our student. Though not

---

[39]Ibid., p. 104.
[40]Ibid., p. 106.
[41]Ibid., p. 107.
[42]Ibid., p. 106.

yet awake, she is—or seems to be—simultaneously aware of two ranges of consciousness. In one, she is experiencing the thrill and intrigue of an adventure; in another, she knows that this is a dream. In one range of consciousness, she is one of the characters; in the other, she is observing it from a position of greater knowledge. In some analogous sense, the incarnate Son has two ranges of consciousness. Morris is aware that this account only gains possibility, and he is well aware of the limitations of the analogy.

The two-minds proposal has drawn criticism. Perhaps the most common and persistent complaint is that it does not do enough to secure the unity of the person. Those philosophers and theologians who take a mind to be identical to a person will inevitably find two persons in Morris's account—and thus a Christology that is guilty of Nestorianism. The precise meaning of "Nestorianism" is important here, and there is a strong case to be made that something akin to Morris's proposal is to be found in patristic theology. But it is not to be found among the Nestorians—rather, it (or something like it in important respects) is found among the proponents of Nicene-Constantinopolitan and Chalcedonian orthodoxy. Nonetheless, however, the basic worry persists. Even if two-minds Christology is not exactly a kind of Nestorianism, and even if it doesn't entail the heretical theory, it simply remains too close to it. Surely, many critics aver, a better model is available elsewhere.

"He emptied himself": Modified kenotic Christology. Some of Morris's friendly critics opt instead for a modified version of kenotic Christology. Drawing inspiration—and its name—from the famous *kenosis* passage, Philippians 2:5-11, kenotic Christology works to resolve the problems remaining for Morris's model by specifying what *emptying* (or "surrendering") means with respect to the incarnation. Kenotic Christologies were fairly prevalent in the nineteenth and (early) twentieth centuries, but the more recent analytic model differs from those in some important respects.[43] Some of these earlier theories (e.g., those

---

[43]For a very helpful discussion of some of these options, see Thomas R. Thompson, "Nineteenth-Century Kenotic Christology: The Waxing, Waning, and Weighing of a Quest for a Coherent Christology," in *Exploring Kenotic Christology: The Self-Emptying of God*, ed. C. Stephen Evans (Oxford: Oxford University Press, 2006), pp. 74-111.

of Thomasius, Ebrard and Martenson) suggested that the Son relinquished some of the divine attributes in the incarnation, and other, and much more radical, theories (e.g., that of Gess) supposed that the Son gave up his *divinity* in the incarnation. The more recent analytic model differs from these earlier theories quite significantly in several respects (thus the label "modified kenotic Christology"), and it should not be confused with them.

The modified analytic approach is represented in the work of Ronald J. Feenstra, Stephen T. Davis and C. Stephen Evans.[44] They are in general agreement with Morris with respect to the overall metaphysical commitments: they posit an abstractist view and help themselves to recent advances in metaphysics. They agree that there is an important distinction between individual-essences and kind-essences, and they hold that the person of Christ has exactly one individual essence and, as incarnate, two kind-essences (humanity and divinity). They agree further with the distinction between being fully human and being merely human, and with classical orthodoxy they insist that Christ is fully human but not merely human. Furthermore, they accept the distinction between common and essential properties. But at this point they adapt Morris's account. For where Morris uses the distinction between common and essential properties to discuss the humanity of Christ, the proponents of modified kenotic Christology (hereafter MKC) also think of terms of common and essential properties of *divinity*. As we have seen, MKC rejects the notion, found in Thomasius, Ebrard, Martenson and Gess, that the Son divested himself of all or even some of the divine attributes. Nonetheless, MKC insists that the kenosis is real—*something* is given up or surrendered in the incarnation (rather than being merely a matter of addition). What is given up is this: the *common* employment of the *essential* divine attributes is surrendered in the kenosis of the incarnation.

Consider the attribute of omniscience. Where the traditional understanding is that omniscience is an essential attribute of divinity, and where the older kenotic models were willing to deny that omniscience is

---

[44]But also see the concretist kenotic model offered by Thomas Senor, "Drawing on Many Traditions: An Ecumenical Kenotic Christology," in *The Metaphysics of the Incarnation*, ed. Anna Marmadoro and Jonathan Hill (Oxford: Oxford University Press, 2011), pp. 88-113.

an essential attribute, MKC insists that what is essential is rather the attribute of *omniscient-unless-kenotically-and-redemptively-incarnate*. This,
rather than omniscience *simpliciter*, is the divine-knowledge attribute. It
is shared between and among the divine persons, all of whom are genuinely *homoousios*. Had the Father or Holy Spirit become incarnate (as
the mainstream tradition insists could have been the case), then the
Father or the Spirit would have exercised this divine attribute as does the
incarnate Son. On the other hand, had the Son not become incarnate, he
would have continued to exercise it just as do the Father and Spirit. But
because the Son, in the economy of salvation, has become incarnate, he
exercises the attribute differently. But note that what he surrenders is a
common divine attribute or property—that of exemplifying the divine-
knowledge attribute in the usual or standard way. He does not, according
to MKC, surrender the essential divine attribute. Even though he employs it in the uncommon way, the Son nonetheless continues to share
this attribute with the Father and Spirit: all are *omniscient-unless-
kenotically-and-redemptively-incarnate*, but only the Son is so incarnate.
So even though the incarnate Son does not have all of the *common* properties of divinity, he does retain all of the *essential* divine attributes.

The proponents of MKC argue that their view offers several important
advantages over both heterodox and more traditional two-minds views.
First, they argue that MKC fits very well with the data of Scripture. At
one level, the model draws inspiration from the famous kenosis passage
of the New Testament.

> In your relationships with one another, have the same mindset as Christ Jesus:
>
> Who, being in very nature God,
>> did not consider equality with God something to be used to his own
>> advantage;
> rather, he made himself nothing
>> by taking the very nature of a servant,
>> being made in human likeness.
> And being found in appearance as a man,
>> he humbled himself
>> by becoming obedient to death—even death on a cross!

> Therefore God exalted him to the highest place
> 　and gave him the name that is above every name,
> that at the name of Jesus every knee should bow,
> 　in heaven and on earth and under the earth,
> and every tongue confess that Jesus Christ is Lord,
> 　to the glory of God the Father. (Phil 2:5-11)

This claim to a foundation in Paul's writings must not be misunderstood. The proponents of MKC do not claim that their view is *demanded* by the proper exegesis of Philippians 2. Their claim is more modest: it is that MKC coheres well with what Paul says here (perhaps it is the *best* fit). More important for the adherents of MKC, however, are the portraits of Jesus in the Gospels. They point out that the Gospel accounts (in John as well as the Synoptics) show Jesus Christ as someone who is divine yet who also is limited in knowledge and expressive of the full and robust range of human emotions (bearing evidence of finitude). In sum, they show a man who is "fully dependent on the Father through the power of the Spirit."[45] It is not as though the two-minds view *cannot* account for texts that speak to the ignorance and limitations of Jesus, but it cannot, defenders of MKC will say, do so nearly as naturally or intuitively as does MKC. As Gordon Fee concludes, "An orthodox biblical Christology almost certainly must embrace some form of a 'kenotic' understanding of the Incarnation, that the One who was truly God, also in his Incarnation lived a truly human life, a life in which he *grew* both in stature and in wisdom and understanding (Luke 2:52), learned obedience through what he suffered (Heb 5:8), and who as Son of the Father did not know the day or the hour (Mark 13:32)."[46] In Davis's view, his "own reasons for following the kenotic route are primarily biblical."[47]

Defenders of MKC also maintain that the view is consistent with classical Christian orthodoxy. They admit that it is not the standard view either of the fathers or doctors of the church; neither the major

---

[45]Gordon Fee, "The New Testament and Kenosis Christology," in Evans, *Exploring Kenotic Christology*, p. 44.

[46]Ibid., p. 43.

[47]Stephen T. Davis, "The Metaphysics of Kenosis," in Marmadoro and Hill, *Metaphysics of the Incarnation*, p. 133.

patristic theologians nor the medieval scholastics teach any form of the view. Nonetheless, its defenders insist, it is formally consistent with the major creeds and councils of orthodoxy. They resolutely deny that it runs afoul of the guidelines laid down by the ecumenical councils, and they likewise deny that it either embraces or entails any of the major heresies. Does it leave orthodoxy in favor of some version of Arianism? No, not at all; it can embrace *homoousios* and reject all forms of Arianism. Does it entail some version of Apollinarianism? No, or at least not obviously so. Moreover, MKC is said to safeguard the unity of the person of Christ. When faced with the question, Does the Son of Man know the day and the hour or does he not know the day and the hour? MKC does not need to resort to a sophisticated or nuanced answer. Neither does it need to do so by way of a strategy that threatens to divide the person of the Son. There is no need to say that "the Son knows it according to his divine mind but not according to his human mind"—thus apparently leaving us without a satisfactory answer to the question, but what does the *person* know? Instead, the answer is as straightforward as the words of Jesus himself: no, he does not know the day or the hour. Finally, the religious appeal of MKC is seen by its proponents as a real strength. As Davis and Evans say, "A kenotic account should increase our wonder and sense of awe that God's love and power should stoop so low for our salvation. A love that so recklessly throws away the privileges and prerogatives of divinity appeals not merely to our intellects but also to our hearts. It offers us a God who is truly Emanuel—God with us, suffering with us, fully embracing the human condition. All for love."[48]

But MKC has drawn criticism. Many critics think that it simply drifts too far from the tradition with respect to its characterization of the essential divine attributes. (The venerable doctrine of divine simplicity stands as a particularly difficult challenge for MKC.) The charge here is not necessarily that MKC runs afoul of the creeds themselves; it is rather that it skews the traditional understanding of the divine attributes. Of course the defenders of MKC are aware of this, and they are not without

---

[48]Stephen T. Davis and C. Stephen Evans, "Conclusion: The Promise of Kenosis," in Evans, *Exploring Kenotic Christology*, p. 321.

response. They argue that the Anselmian method does not have the last word and that we should be willing to revise our intuitively prior beliefs in light of God's revelation. And since Scripture seems to show a Jesus who grows in knowledge but is still ignorant, then we should adapt out beliefs accordingly. So, Feenstra concludes, MKC not only follows a proper method, but also follows it to the proper conclusion: Christians should be willing to revise their positions—even deeply traditional ones—in light of revelation, and biblical portrayals of Jesus Christ demand just that kind of revision. So even though the proponents admit that MKC is nontraditional in some ways, they nonetheless insist that it is consistent with the creeds and indeed *more* faithful to Scripture.

Other critics worry that MKC promotes solutions that are simply too ad hoc or "gerrymandered."[49] Its defenders might grant the point that what they offer is unusual, but, they can insist, the incarnation itself is radically unusual and surprising. Should we be all that surprised if our preconceived theological notions need some adjustment in light of this amazing event? Thomas Senor, however, sharpens the criticism; he argues that the divine attributes of MKC are not "suitably deep" or "fundamental."[50] Still other critics (even those who are sympathetic) worry that MKC is yet unstable. For if MKC is correct, then all divine persons have the attribute of being omniscient-unless-kenotically-and-redemptively-incarnate. But if, as the tradition holds is possible, the divine persons were to all become incarnate (simultaneously), then it seems as though no divine person would be omniscient—and thus omniscience would be contingent rather than necessary and thus not essential to divinity after all. If the defender of MKC were to try to avoid this problem by denying that the Father or Spirit could become incarnate, then it is hard indeed to know what even to make of the claim that they share the attribute of being omniscient-unless-kenotically-and-redemptively-incarnate. In addition, MKC would now face another dilemma: if only the Son has the ability to become incarnate, then the Son has the ability to do something that neither Father nor Spirit can do. If so, then it is hard

---

[49]J. P. Moreland and William Lane Craig, *Philosophical Foundations for a Christian Worldview* (Downers Grove, IL: InterVarsity Press, 2003), p. 607.
[50]Senor, "An Ecumenical Kenotic Christology," p. 107.

to see how they could be omnipotent—or how the Son could be *homoousios* with the Father and Spirit.[51] Taken either way, then, it is not obvious that MKC is as promising as it first appears. At the same time, however, it would be wrong to reject it as formally heterodox.

Concretist accounts: Qua-moves and specification. So far we have discussed two prominent abstractist proposals, but not all christological models work with an abstractist account. Much of the Christian tradition works with a concretist metaphysics, and the view has distinguished contemporary defenders as well.[52] Where abstractists take the natures to be properties, concretists take them to be reified. While concretists do not deny that there are abstract natures such as caninity, equinity or humanity, when talking about specific, concrete natures they are concerned not about the full set of properties individually necessary and jointly sufficient to be a dog or a horse but with the caninity of the dog Hershey, the equinity of Smoky the Cowhorse or the humanity of Socrates. As Joseph Jedwab explains, "On the view known as Abstractism, the Son comes to have an abstract human nature by becoming a concrete human nature, but not by assuming a distinct concrete human nature. On the view known as Concretism, by contrast, the Son comes to have an abstract human nature by assuming a distinct concrete human nature."[53]

On the classical Aristotelian metaphysics inherited by the medieval scholastics, every primary substance (e.g., Hershey the chocolate Labrador, Smoky the Cowhorse or Socrates) has a secondary substance-kind (e.g., caninity, equinity or humanity) that pertains to it and without which it could not exist: every horse has the substance-kind equinity and could not exist without it. Marilyn McCord Adams helpfully explains that "for every primary substance *x*, there is *only one* secondary substance-kind *K* that pertains to *x* through itself and is essential to it, in the sense

---

[51]See Thomas H. McCall and Keith D. Yandell, "On Trinitarian Subordinationism," *Philosophia Christi* (2009): 355-56.

[52]The ranks of important contemporary concretists include Oliver D. Crisp, Marilyn McCord Adams, Brian Leftow and Eleonore Stump.

[53]Joseph Jedwab, "The Incarnation and Unity of Consciousness," in Marmadoro and Hill, *Metaphysics of the Incarnation*, p. 169.

that x could not exist without being a K."[54] The reception of standard Aristotelian metaphysics presents an immediate challenge to Christian orthodoxy, however, for according to Aristotelian essentialism, no primary substance can have more than one secondary substance (or substance-kind). Medieval theologians did not flinch with respect to their commitment to Christian orthodoxy, but nor did they reject Aristotelianism. Instead, they worked to make important modifications to the metaphysics of Aristotle. Adams explains that for medieval theology, "it is possible for a primary substance x that is essentially of a substance-kind also to possess/be/come to be of substance-kind K' (where K is not the same as K') contingently and non-essentially."[55] The medieval theologians insisted not only on the distinction between primary substances (Hershey the chocolate Labrador, Smoky the Cowhorse and Socrates) and substance-kinds (caninity, equinity and humanity) but also of both from individual substance-natures (*Hershey's* caninity, *Smoky's* equinity and *Socrates's* humanity). They are happy to grant that Aristotle is right insofar as he describes the normal or default position, for in most cases a primary substance has one and only one individual substance-nature; Hershey has only Hershey's caninity, Smoky has only Smoky's equinity and Socrates has only his humanity. But they also deny that this is *necessarily* the case, for it is not obvious that an individual substance-nature either must be ontologically independent or cannot be united with another. In the incarnation this is exactly what has happened: the concrete human nature is assumed by Christ and is ontologically dependent on the Logos, who assumes it.

So far the various concretist proposals are generally agreed. But what we have said to this point only lays the groundwork for the important steps forward, and so far little has been said that might help to deal with the common objections and challenges to the traditional doctrine. Concretists disagree among themselves about the details, but many affirm some kind of part-whole (or "mereological") model of the incarnation. Perhaps the most famous of the proponents of this view is Thomas

---

[54]Marilyn McCord Adams, *Christ and Horrors: The Coherence of Christology* (Cambridge: Cambridge University Press, 2006), p. 111.
[55]Ibid., p. 112.

Aquinas. He considers the question, Was Christ a creature? and answers by noting that the Arians say that Christ is a creature and "less than his Father"; of course Aquinas also knows that Christ is fully human. He replies in this way: "We must not say absolutely that Christ is a creature or less than his Father; but with a qualification, viz. in his human nature." He explains further that "such things as could not be considered to belong to the divine person in itself may be predicated simply of God by reason of his human nature; thus we say simply that Christ suffered, died and was buried: even as in corporeal and human beings, things of which we may doubt whether they belong to the whole or the part."[56] This is because "whether they belong to the whole or the part, if they are observed to exist in a part, are not predicated of the whole simply, i.e. without qualification, for we do not say that the Ethiopian is white but that he is white as regards his teeth; but we say without qualification that he is curly, since this can only belong to him as regards his hair."[57]

Adams describes this "qualification" as "specification": the relevant part is specified. A descriptive statement could refer to a part, several parts or the whole. Each descriptive statement (or "predication") must be closely analyzed, but with such analysis we can make sense of statements such as "God began to exist and was born in time" and "God suffered under Pontius Pilate and died on the cross"—and we can do so with a classically Christian doctrine of God intact. What we mean by such claims is not that God *simpliciter* was born or died; what we mean is that God *the Son* was born and died. Neither do we mean that the person of the Son was born or died *simpliciter*; instead we mean that God the Son began to exist and suffered death *according to his human nature*. According to this strategy (also known as the "reduplicative strategy"— roughly, the strategy of saying that "Christ *as God* has this property, *as man* its complement"),[58] Eleonore Stump explains, "the fact that both limited and unlimited power are attributed to Christ does not show the Chalcedonian formula of the incarnation to be incoherent, because om-

---

[56]Thomas Aquinas, *Summa Theologica* IIIa.16.8, trans. by the Fathers of the Dominican Province (New York: Benzinger Brothers, 1948).

[57]Adams, *Christ and Horrors*, pp. 130-33.

[58]So Morris, *Logic of God Incarnate*, p. 38.

nipotence is predicated of Christ in his divine nature and lack of omnipotence is predicated of him in his human nature."[59] So "Christ *qua*
God is omnipotent; *qua* human, he is not."[60]

A noted contemporary defender of this approach, Brian Leftow,
argues that God the Son (the second person of the Holy Trinity) exists
eternally and necessarily but is joined with a concrete human nature
(a body and soul) in the incarnation. Combining God the Son and the
human body and soul renders one composed entity: Jesus Christ. The
human body and soul now becomes a part of Jesus Christ, but it does
not become part of God the Son (per se). As he explains, while the
body and soul are joined to God the Son, "they do not become part of"
him. God the Son "does not come to consist of hands, feet, etc."; rather,
he now "has hands, feet, etc. grafted on."[61] Leftow wrestles with worries
that his view seems Nestorian, and he admits that there are important
metaphysical differences between us and the incarnate Son of God. But
he insists that this is true of *any* (orthodox) account of incarnation, and
he concludes that, even though Jesus Christ is an unusual human, he
is nonetheless fully human.[62]

Stump recognizes that such a strategy, however popular in the
Christian tradition, is unpopular today because it is seen to offer a merely
semantic "solution" that leaves the real problem intact. But she argues
that the view is defensible nonetheless (given a proper understanding of
parts, wholes and their properties). On Aquinas's view, as she explains it,
"there is a distinction between a property a whole has in its own right and
a property it has in virtue of having a constituent that has that property
in its own right," and "a whole can borrow a property from one of its
constituents."[63] Drawing on the molecule CAT/enhancer-binding
protein (C/EBP) as an example, she argues that we can see this clearly.
C/EBP "is a dimer, each of whose subunits is a protein which is coiled in

---

[59]Eleonore Stump, "Aquinas' Metaphysics of the Incarnation," in *The Incarnation: An Interdisci-plinary Symposium on the Incarnation of the Son of God*, ed. Stephen T. Davis, Daniel Kendall, SJ, and Gerald O'Collins, SJ (Oxford: Oxford University Press, 2002), p. 211.

[60]Ibid.

[61]Brian Leftow, "The Humanity of God," in Marmadoro and Hill, *Metaphysics of the Incarnation*, p. 22. Leftow does not offer further explanation of what "grafted on" means.

[62]Ibid.

[63]Stump, "Aquinas' Metaphysics of the Incarnation," p. 212.

an alpha helix coil. The molecule thus has the property of being coiled in the alpha helix manner, but it has that property in virtue of the fact that it has two parts which are coiled in that way. Each of these parts of the molecule, however, is coiled in the alpha helix manner in its own right. On the other hand, the whole molecule has the property of regulating DNA transcription, and this property it has in its own right."[64] At the same time, C/EBP "is a conglomerate of two such dimer units which bend away from each other in a limp Y-shape at one end of the molecule."[65] What this yields is the conclusion that while it is true that C/EBP "'*qua* dimer with coiled subunits has the property of being coiled in the alpha helix manner' predicates a property of the whole molecule which it borrows from a part" (a part that has it in its own right), it is also true that C/EBP "*qua* Y-shaped is not coiled in the alpha helix manner."[66] Analogously, the incarnate Son has some properties qua human nature and has other properties qua divine nature. Stump thus concludes that, when suitably understood, this model serves to remove the threat of contradiction from the orthodox doctrine.

Thomas P. Flint, a very sympathetic critic of mereological concretist models, raises several worries. He is concerned that at least some versions of this model face the threat of loss of identity, for in worlds in which the Logos is incarnate he combines with a concrete human nature (body and soul) to compose the Son, while in worlds in which the Logos does not become incarnate he is simply the Son (sans humanity). But if this is true, then, given a classical account of identity, the person who is the incarnate Son is not identical to the person who is the Son. Surely this is a problem.[67] In addition, this model seems to "insulate" the person of the Son too much (as if his humanity, worn like a jacket or spacesuit, collects all the dirt and protects him from genuine contact with the world). Flint asks: has this not "so insulated the Son from humanity as to call into question the very meaning of the incarnation?"[68]

---

[64]Ibid., p. 205.

[65]Ibid., p. 213.

[66]Ibid., pp. 212-13.

[67]Thomas P. Flint, "Should Concretists Part with Mereological Models of the Incarnation?," in Marmadoro and Hill, *Metaphysics of the Incarnation*, p. 73.

[68]Ibid., p. 81.

And are we not still threatened with the specter of two agents—even two *persons*? What is this if not a version of Nestorianism?[69]

The defenders of mereological concretism are not unaware of the challenges, and they are not without reply. Oliver D. Crisp and others have considered these (and additional) objections. Taking them in reverse order, it is important to see that worries about Nestorianism are heightened by concretist explanations. But while the concretist Christologian can admit that some of the common language (of "Christ's human nature" as the ready-made composite of body and soul) may *sound like* Nestorianism (or some kind of quasi-Nestorianism) to modern ears, it is not at all obvious that the model itself falls outside the bounds of creedal orthodoxy. When we turn our attention to the "insulation problem," it is important to be clear about just what is and what is not implied by the model itself. The model itself does not require that the divine nature is hermetically sealed off from the human nature, and a theologian who is not committed to, say, such classical understandings of the divine attributes as simplicity and impassibility could maintain the model. In other words, there is nothing about the model itself that stipulates just what properties are transferred (from the part to the whole, or from one part to another). But it is also important to see that the fact that this model can be taken to support a robust doctrine of the incarnation while still remaining committed to the doctrines of the classical tradition is hardly a stain on its orthodoxy. At any rate it is hard indeed to see how this could be a stumbling block to someone committed to the coherence of a doctrine that is creedally orthodox.

But what of the objection that mereological models entail that the person of the incarnate Son is no longer identical with the person who just is the Son? The main worry seems to be that if the Logos and the human nature of Christ *combine* to form God the Son, then—given classical identity—either God the Son-as-incarnate-Christ is not identical to God the Son or the humanity is necessary (*de re*) and thus essential to the Son. In other words, either God the Son would not be identical to Jesus Christ or the humanity is necessary and essential to God the Son.

---

[69]E.g., Thomas Senor, "The Compositional Account of the Incarnation," *Faith and Philosophy* (2007): 53.

So what are we to make of this? Well, if the Logos and the human nature (body and soul) of Christ really do combine to form the eternal Son, then there may be a problem. But the concretist proponent of classical orthodoxy need not hold that the humanity contributes to the composition of *the Son*. Indeed, the concretist *should not* do so. The Logos (who *is*, in the classical sense of identity, the eternal Son of the Father) combines with the human nature to form Jesus Christ. So the person who is the Son is Jesus Christ, and this is what is required by creedal orthodoxy.

Some concretists (perhaps most famously John Duns Scotus) are quite sensitive to such concerns and think more explicitly in terms of a "subject-accident" model of the incarnation. Subject-accident models also work with a version of reduplication, but they deny also that this is *mere* reduplication. With the other concretist (and abstractist) proposals, subject-accident concretists also think that Christ qua divinity is eternal and has necessary existence but qua humanity is born in time and exists contingently. But on this account the qua phrase works, in the words of Marilyn Adams, because it "distracts the predicate."[70] Thus "the Ethiopian is white with respect to his teeth" does not entail that the predicate is white; "whiteness" does not describe the Ethiopian (without proper qualification). What is entailed is not the conclusion that the Ethiopian is white; what is entailed rather is this: the Ethiopian is "white-toothed." But nor are we simply talking about the tooth itself; as Richard Cross puts it, "The Ethiopian, not his tooth, is white-toothed."[71] Thus "Christ qua human" is a creature, but this does not entail that Christ *is* a creature. It only entails that the humanity of Christ is created. Some critics may still worry that the subject-accident model, for all its sophistication, still fails the test of Chalcedonian orthodoxy because it seems to imply that the divine Word does not have the human nature in the same way that *we* have the human nature. But surely on just any orthodox Christology we should not conclude that Christ has humanity *just like* the rest of us. For here the concretist, as well as the abstractist, can appeal to Morris's distinctions. In doing so, the concretist defender can insist that the creeds only teach that Christ is *essentially* human (rather than *merely*

---

[70]Adams, *Christ and Horrors*, p. 133.
[71]Cross, *Metaphysics of the Incarnation*, p. 204.

human), and while it surely is a *common* property of humanity to have human nature in the "normal" way, this does not amount to an onto-logical requirement that it is an *essential* property. In other words, what is essential to Christ is *being human*, not *being merely human* or *being human in the normal way* (whatever, exactly, the "normal" human way really is). Adams concludes that, on this concretist view, the divine Logos is the ultimate subject of the human actions of Christ because of the ontological dependence of the humanity on the divine Logos; predi-cation is thus of the person of the Word according to the nature. "In general, 'the divine Word is *F-qua*-Divine and not-*F-qua*-human' seems both to keep characterization and to avoid contradiction! Was not this the desired result?"[72]

Conclusion. It should be plain from the foregoing that there is no clear consensus on the way forward, and that work in Christology is not yet done. As Cross says, "Modern discussion in philosophical theology on the doctrine of the Incarnation still represents to some extent work in progress."[73] There are many issues that still warrant consideration: the question of whether or not Christ assumed a "fallen" human nature, issues related to the "necessity" and "fittingness" of the incarnation, the doctrines of the virginal conception and bodily ascension, and the re-lation of the person to the "work" of Christ (to name but a few) all cry out for further investigation.[74] There is nothing approaching unanimity about the best way forward in understanding the metaphysics of the incarnation. At the same time, however, we should recognize the vi-brancy and compelling nature of the doctrine. Efforts to demonstrate its incoherence are yet unsuccessful; indeed, as we have seen, there is more than one way to turn back the objections while satisfying the desiderata of orthodoxy. Moreover, the religious power and compelling nature of the doctrine remains powerful indeed. But are the options so wide open

---

[72]Adams, *Christ and Horrors*, p. 133. For some of the remaining worries about Adams's proposal, see Michael C. Rea, introduction to *Oxford Readings in Philosophical Theology*, vol. 1, *Trinity, Incarnation, and Atonement*, ed. Michael C. Rea (Oxford: Oxford University Press, 2009), p. 13.

[73]Richard Cross, "The Incarnation," in Flint and Rea, *Oxford Handbook of Philosophical Theology*, p. 470.

[74]See the list of Gerald O'Collins, "The Incarnation: Critical Issues," in Davis, Kendall and O'Collins, *The Incarnation*, pp. 1-27.

that virtually anything can count as an orthodox option? Or are there ways that the history of doctrine might guide and discipline our christological work?

"I AM MY BODY, BROKEN FOR YOU"?
PHYSICALIST CHRISTOLOGY AS A CASE STUDY

While the last case study showed how analytic theology informed by the tradition of Christian doctrine has the resources to respond to criticisms of the classical doctrine of the incarnation, this one takes a different tack: this case study shows how analytic theology that is informed by classical Christian orthodoxy might seek to question and correct a recent analytic proposal.

Merricks's physicalist Christology. The doctrine of the incarnation stands at the heart of historic Christian faith. For centuries Christians have taken this to mean that the eternal Logos, the second person of the Holy Trinity, became human without ceasing to be divine. The Chalcedonian Formula provides a historic expression of this doctrine. As Brian Leftow summarizes the doctrinal claim, "Chalcedonian orthodoxy has it that this involves one person, God the Son, having two natures, divine and human."[75] Such claims raise all sorts of questions, of course, and they generate various metaphysical models of the possibility of incarnation.

One recent and very interesting proposal is this: in the incarnation, the Son is identical with the *body* of Jesus Christ. Trenton Merricks argues forcefully for this claim. Merricks recognizes that "compositionalist" models are "arguably the historically dominant theory," but he dismisses them because he has a hard time seeing how the such accounts might avoid Nestorianism (because he cannot see how the individual human nature assumed by Christ could fail to be a separate person).[76] As a convinced physicalist, he is certain that the incarnate Son "has a body in the same sense that you and I do" and indeed is related to his body just as all humans are related to their bodies.[77] In addition to other

---

[75]Leftow, "Humanity of God," p. 20.

[76]Trenton Merricks, "Dualism, Physicalism, and the Incarnation," in *Persons, Human and Divine*, ed. Peter van Inwagen and Dean Zimmerman (Oxford: Oxford University Press, 2007), p. 282 n. 1.

[77]Ibid., p. 282.

reasons for rejecting mind-body dualism,[78] he thinks that the incarnation itself "casts doubt on dualism."[79] Instead, Merricks endorses physicalist Christology: "You have a body if and only if you are identical with that body. I assume that, in the Incarnation, God the Son is related to the body of Jesus just as you and I are related to our respective bodies. So, given physicalism, God the Son, in the Incarnation, is identical with the body of Jesus. That is, in becoming a human, he became a body."[80]

Being identical with the body does not entail that there are no mental properties; Merricks thinks that his version of physicalism is consistent with "property dualism."[81] Nonetheless, physicalism "makes becoming identical with (and so having) a body necessary for becoming human."[82] He concludes that "the Incarnation points us toward physicalism," and this "gives Christians good reasons to be physicalists."[83]

In what follows, I argue that Merricks's conclusion is much too hasty. Significant theological questions remain open for the proponent of Merricksian physicalist Christology, and more work needs to be done before his conclusion is established. Although his criticisms of dualist Christology are interesting and important, I do not focus on them here.[84] Instead, I raise two broad challenges for Merricks's proposal: more needs to be done to show that it is indeed coherent, and more needs to be done to show that it can be orthodox as well as coherent.

Some worries about coherence. Merricks claims that God the Son (GS) just *is* identical with the body of Jesus Christ (B) in the incarnation.[85] Alvin Plantinga worries about such physicalist Christology. He points out that "prior to the Incarnation, however, the second person of the

---

[78]E.g., Trenton Merricks, "The Resurrection of the Body and the Life Everlasting," in *Reason for the Hope Within*, ed. Michael J. Murray (Grand Rapids: Eerdmans, 1999), pp. 261-86.

[79]Merricks, "Dualism, Physicalism, and the Incarnation," p. 292.

[80]Ibid., p. 294.

[81]Ibid., p. 295.

[82]Ibid., p. 298.

[83]Ibid., p. 299.

[84]On these criticisms, see Jessica Wilson, "Physicalism and the Incarnation," (unfortunately) unpublished paper; and Luke Van Horn, "Merricks's Soulless Savior," *Faith and Philosophy* (2010): 330-41.

[85]Merricks, "Dualism, Physicalism, and the Incarnation," pp. 294-95. Merricks also says that "physicalism makes *becoming* identical with (and so having) a body necessary for becoming human," p. 298 (emphasis mine). The language of *becoming* identical raises other worries about coherence, but I shall not deal with those here.

Trinity was not a material object, but an immaterial being. If, however, as materialists assert, to be a human being is to be a material object, then the second person of the Trinity must have become a material object. . . . But then an immaterial being became a material object; and this seems to me to be impossible."[86] For as it is "clearly impossible" for "the number seven or the proposition that $7 + 5 = 12$, or the property of self-exemplification, all of which are immaterial objects, should become, turn into, material objects," so also it is "less clearly impossible, but still impossible, it seems to me, that the second person of the Trinity—that personal being with will and intellect and affections—should turn into a material object."[87] Brian Leftow agrees; he is convinced that "materialist christologies are non-starters," for it seems "flatly impossible" for something "relevantly like a soul" to become "relevantly like a stone."[88]

While neither Leftow nor Plantinga spells out his concerns in great detail, it isn't terribly hard to see at least the appearances of some problems here. If identity is behaving itself and is reflexive, transitive and symmetric, it is an equivalence relation that satisfies Leibniz's law of the indiscernibility of identicals:

(LL) For any objects x and y, if x and y are identical, then for any property P, x has P if and only if y has P.

$(\forall x)\ (\forall y)\ [x = y => (\forall P)\ (P(x) <=> P(y))]$

So if GS and B really are identical, then if GS has some property P, then B will also have P.

$[GS = B => (\forall P)\ (P(GS) <=> P(B))]$

And, of course, if B has some property P^*, then GS will also have that P^*. We don't have to look far to see trouble looming. Presumably, as the second person of the Trinity, GS has the attributes of aseity and eternal (or everlasting) existence; we can say that GS has the property E: *enjoys a beginningless and eternal existence*. But if GS has this, and if GS really

---

[86]Alvin Plantinga, "On Heresy, Mind, and Truth," *Faith and Philosophy* (1999): 186.
[87]Ibid.
[88]Leftow, "Humanity of God," p. 21.

is identical to B, then B must also have *E*. On the other hand, the human B presumably exists dependently, and surely B—*this* physical object or organism—has come into existence. Consider a property such as *W*: *began to exist as an embryo in the womb of Mary*. Presumably, B has *W*. And if GS is identical to B, then GS must also have *W*. But it isn't exactly a stretch to think that *E* and *W* are contradictory—if so, then if GS has *W*, then GS cannot have *E*.[89] We could pile up these examples—GS exists necessarily while B exists contingently; GS is omniscient while B has limited knowledge; GS is omnipotent while B cannot bench-press more than, say, 456 pounds; GS is omnipresent while B is physically limited (and, say, only 5'6" and 143 pounds); GS is immaterial while B is material; and so on. The basic worry should be obvious.

There is, of course, a fairly standard way to employ and understand such locutions as "X became Y." On this view, when we say that "X became Y," we don't mean that X became identical to Y. Instead, we pre-suppose metaphysical identity and then talk about various kinds of changes. Presupposing the identity of X and Y, we are only talking about change (over times and, perhaps, worlds). We only mean something like "the boy became a football player in addition to being a baseball player" or "the boy gave up on baseball and started playing football" or "the second baseman is now the quarterback" (or even perhaps something like "the boy playing football could have been a soccer player").[90] Accordingly, since GS = B, and since GS clearly has *E*, then it really isn't correct to say that GS has *W*. Or, if we insist on saying that GS has *W*, what we really mean is this: the Son did *not* begin to exist *simpliciter* but instead *began to exist-in-the-womb-of-Mary*; the Son did not come into existence in Mary's womb but only "moved into" her womb and began to exist *there*.[91]

Taken this way (as, I think, we should), when Merricks claims that GS

---

[89]Whatever challenges may face classical Christology (concretist and compositional), at least it has ready-made ways (e.g., "specification") to respond to these concerns.

[90]One way to do this is by modifying "Leibniz's law" (of the indiscernibility of identicals) to account for change across times and worlds. See Michael J. Loux, introduction to *The Possible and the Actual: Readings in the Metaphysics of Modality*, ed. Michael J. Loux (Ithaca, NY: Cornell University Press, 1979), pp. 42-43.

[91]As Mike Rea has pointed out to me, Merricks's view entails that "embryo" is (at least in this case) a phase-sortal.

is identical with B, he really would mean that the entity that is always and already identical to GS has changed from ~B into B. The Son was GS-as-~B and then changed into GS-as-B. In possible worlds (and at the appropriate time segments therein) wherein GS is incarnate, GS changes into B. Perhaps this move will help; maybe it will alleviate worries about incoherence. So GS is omniscient but B isn't omniscient (see Mk 13:34)? Well, GS is omniscient in some possible worlds (and times)—but not when he becomes B. So, for instance, at the appropriate times in the galaxy of possible worlds wherein GS is incarnate, GS is not omniscient but knows only what a first-century Jew (with B's brain and normal education) might know, but in other possible worlds (or at preincarnate times in this one) GS is omniscient.

Does such a strategy help Merricks's proposal? Maybe. But it is far from obvious that this understanding of the "identity" claim will really satisfy Merricks's theological desiderata, for none of us are related to our bodies in this way. On Merricks's view, none of us, that is, preexist our bodily existence as nonphysical. But GS does. On physicalism, there are no persons who preexist their bodies; there are no persons who are—or ever were—distinct from their bodies. But on physicalist Christology, there is a person (GS) who preexists his body and who is—or, more appropriately, *was*—distinct from his body. So then how might it be the case that "God the Son, in virtue of being incarnate, is related to his body just as you and I are related to our respective bodies" or "is related to his body just as each and every other human is related to his or her body"?[92]

Alternatively, perhaps we should adopt perdurantism and think in terms of, say, worm-theory.[93] Accordingly, GS is identical to the entire GS-as-~B through GS-as-B continuum; earlier temporal parts of GS are ~B while later temporal parts of GS are B. But this doesn't seem all that promising either, for on this account it isn't obvious just how GS could,

---

[92]Merricks, "Dualism, Physicalism, and the Incarnation," pp. 281-82.

[93]On worm theory (and four dimensionalism more generally), see Michael C. Rea, "The Metaphysics of Original Sin," in *Persons: Human and Divine*, ed. Peter van Inwagen and Dean Zimmerman (Oxford: Oxford University Press, 2007), pp. 335-38; Michael C. Rea, "Four Dimensionalism," in *The Oxford Handbook of Metaphysics*, ed. Michael J. Loux and Dean W. Zimmerman (Oxford: Oxford University Press, 2003), pp. 246-80; Theodore Sider, "Four-Dimensionalism," *Philosophical Review* (1997): 197-231; Sider, *Four-Dimensionalism* (Oxford: Oxford University Press, 2001).

strictly speaking, be identical to B (if GS is identical to the entire GS-as-~B through GS-as-B continuum, then he isn't identical to some temporal part of it).[94] But if he isn't identical to B, then he isn't related to his body just as we are. Thus once again we would fail to satisfy Merricks's crucial desiderata.

Surely more work remains for the christological physicalist. Given *enough* theological adjustments, perhaps it can be made coherent. But caution is in order: given *too many* theological adjustments, it will be much harder to square this physicalist Christology with Chalcedon.

Some theological questions: Physicalist Christology and Chalcedon's letter. Merricks informs us that he intends to stay within the parameters of the Chalcedonian Definition.[95] Clearly, he wants his christological proposal to be not only coherent and meaningful but also theologically orthodox.[96] This is where things start to get theologically interesting. Here are several areas that warrant further consideration.[97]

For catholic orthodoxy, GS must remain *GS* even as he is B. If GS *changes into* B in such a way that there is no more GS and only B, then Jesus Christ is not divine at all and there is no incarnation to talk about. The same divine GS that preexists B must remain divine even as he is B. But how are we to understand the divine nature as the *divine nature of B*? Merricks allows that physical persons can have nonphysical properties; his brand of physicalism will countenance mental properties (and thus is consistent with "property dualism").[98] Merricks rightfully rejects out of hand any view that would entail that B generates the divinity.[99] He suggests that we may possess properties that are neither physical nor mental, and the same would be true of the incarnate Son.[100] In thinking about the relation of B to the divine nature, however, we are not left with much direction.

The Chalcedonian Formula famously includes these denials: *without*

---

[94]As Van Horn argues, "Merricks's Soulless Savior," p. 339.
[95]Merricks, "Dualism, Physicalism, and the Incarnation," p. 281.
[96]Ibid., pp. 292-93.
[97]Apollinarianism has gotten the lion's share of the attention to this point. See Oliver D. Crisp, *God Incarnate: Explorations in Christology* (New York: T & T Clark, 2009), pp. 137-54.
[98]Merricks, "Dualism, Physicalism, and the Incarnation," p. 295.
[99]Ibid., p. 283 n. 5.
[100]Ibid., p. 295.

confusion, without change, without division, without separation. Merricks's Christology is not sufficiently developed to help us a lot here. Perhaps it will mature, but at this point it isn't easy to know just what to make of it. But here are some questions. Consider the *without confusion* phrase—the divine nature and the human nature of Christ are not confused. They are distinct, and their properties remain so. But if, in the incarnation, there is *just B*, then what else is there to Jesus beyond his humanity? Recall that Merricks says that physical persons can have mental properties that cannot be reduced to physical properties, and he says further that both Jesus and the rest of us may also have some properties that are neither physical nor mental. So perhaps even though B is all that there is to the human nature of the incarnate Son, this incarnate Son retains the divine nature as well. But Merricks doesn't say much about any of this, so it is hard to know just what to make of it. If GS = B (in the incarnation), then does B enjoy omnipresence? So: what does it mean to say that the natures are not confused?

Or consider the famous statement that the natures of Christ are *without change.* This is clarified by the addition of the phrase "the difference of the natures being by no means taken away because of the union, but rather the distinctive character of each nature being preserved." On Merricks's proposal, we don't yet know what this means. But surely it would be good to count the cost before concluding that physicalist Christology is superior to other models, and affirmations of the obvious superiority of physicalist Christology over its dualist cousins seem premature indeed in the absence of such cost-counting and price-comparison. So: what does it mean to say that the natures of Christ are without change for physicalist Christology?

Perhaps physicalist Christology can abide by the letter of the Chalcedonian law, and perhaps it can do so with an acceptable doctrine of God yet intact. (Perhaps whether this can be done, and just what this doctrine of God would be, should remain an open question.) Maybe it can even honor the spirit of Chalcedon. Even so, it isn't yet clear that it will handle all puzzles about (apparently) contradictory properties. Clearly, more work awaits.

A theological concern: Physicalist Christology and the resurrection of Jesus. Merricks says that GS must be related to B just as you and I are related to our bodies. He also says this about physical death: "Physicalism suggests that a person does not exist between death and resurrection."[101] Elsewhere, in work focused on resurrection, he says, "So if I am right, you will cease to exist when you die, and then, on the Day of Resurrection, you will come back into existence."[102] What would this mean for Christology? At first glance, it would seem to suggest that the Son no longer even exists after he breathes his last—when he says, "Into your hands I commit my spirit" (Lk 23:46), that's it for him. For if GS really is identical to B, and B no longer exists, then GS no longer exists "either." On this account, there could be no *descensus*. There could be no *extra Calvinisticum* (or *extra Catholicum*).[103] There could be no continuing incarnation of the Son while in the grave. There could be no meaning to Christ's words of hope and promise to the thief on the cross: "today you will be with me in paradise" (Lk 23:43). And there could be no Trinity—at least not from Christ's death until his resurrection, and at least not necessarily. For if GS = B, and B does not exist, then GS does not exist either; if "a person" who is identical with the second person of the Trinity does not exist, then the second person of the Holy Trinity does not exist.

But Merricks also offers this suggestion: "But perhaps a physical person—a human organism—could become non-physical (and presumably non-human) at death and continue to exist in such a state until becoming physical again at the resurrection."[104] Such a suggestion is puzzling *in excelsis* (taken as an expression of physicalism). If a person could

---

[101]Ibid., p. 295 n. 18.

[102]Merricks, "Resurrection of the Body," p. 284 n. 24. Merricks also says that "if we are identical with our bodies, then we do not exist when our bodies do not exist. Therefore, if physicalism is true, at some point between death and the total decay of one's body, one literally ceases to exist," p. 284. It isn't entirely obvious just how this fits with his other statements, but perhaps the "at some point between" is important here for Christology—maybe the three days in the grave are within the crucial time period.

[103]This refers to the insistence by Reformed theologians (following the catholic tradition) that the Logos transcends the human nature of Christ in and during the incarnation. As Richard A. Muller summarizes the point, "The Reformed argued that the Word is fully united to but never totally contained within the human nature and, therefore, even in incarnation is to be conceived as beyond or outside of (*extra*) the human nature," *Dictionary of Latin and Greek Theological Terms: Drawn Principally from Protestant Scholastic Theology* (Grand Rapids: Baker, 1985), p. 111.

[104]Merricks, "Dualism, Physicalism, and the Incarnation," p. 295 n. 18.

become nonphysical but remain human, then are we not seeing physicalism run up the white flag? Merricks seems to see this, and he seems reticent to grant so much (thus the "and presumably non-human"). On the other hand, if the person becomes both nonphysical and nonhuman, then we are left to wonder what in this world (or any other) that entity might be. On this proposal, a physical person or human organism would only be contingently physical and accidentally human rather than essentially so. And it surely wouldn't be the case that this person really is identical with the body at all. For if the person has some property S: *survives the dissolution of the body* but the body does not have S, then the person and the body are not identical. Moreover, the person would only be accidentally related to the body. Surely this isn't good news for physicalism.

Returning to the distinctly christological concerns, it seems that the Son would not be incarnate between the crucifixion and resurrection. He still exists (again as GS *simpliciter*), but he is no longer incarnate. Whatever exactly the penitent thief will consist of after he breathes his last, when Jesus says "today you will be with me in paradise" he clearly cannot mean "*you*-as-a-human-person will be with me." Nor can he mean "you will be with *me as Jesus*" (but rather "me as disincarnate GS"). The resurrection would, then, amount to a literal *re-incarnation.*

Some concluding observations. I take it that various metaphysical proposals may be consistent with classical, creedal orthodoxy. Surely some metaphysical proposals and systems are not congenial to Christianity, but it isn't the case that commitment to Christian orthodoxy demands concomitant commitment to a particular, full-blown metaphysical system (Platonism, Aristotelianism, etc.). What I say here should not be taken as an instance of heresy hunting or anything of the like. In point of fact, I am not entirely unsympathetic to Christian physicalism; though not yet convinced, I am alert to some of the worries about dualism. Some of what Merricks says about the resurrection of the body and the life everlasting (in general) is appealing to me. Nonetheless, Merricks's confident pronouncements about the superiority of physicalist Christology strike me as very premature. Significant theological questions remain open for the proponent of physicalist Christology, and more work—indeed, *much* more work—needs to be done before we can accept Merricksian Christology. We don't yet know whether the view is even coherent, and we sure don't know that it can be both coherent and orthodox.

CONCLUSION

In this chapter, I have outlined some ways in which the Christian tradition might function in analytic theology. Through the use of our christological case studies, I have tried to illustrate some ways that analytic theology might help us to gain a better understanding and defense of classical christological claims, and I have also used them to show how the creedal and confessional statements of classical Christology might curb or correct some speculative christological proposals.

4

Analytic Theology for the Church and the World

Theology is a function of the church.

KARL BARTH

ANALYTIC THEOLOGY AND THE BROADER ASPIRATIONS OF CHRISTIAN THEOLOGY

Nicholas Wolterstorff notes that "there remains in the theologian the longing—admirable in my view—to speak to the world, indeed; to heal the world."[1] I think that what he says about theologians is true. And what he says about theologians *should* be true. Theologians should want to speak to the world. They should long for the healing of the world. Accordingly, analytic theologians should share these concerns. As theologians, they should shoulder these burdens. And they should do so gladly. This means, of course, that the work of analytic theology cannot exist for its own sake. To the contrary, it plays a role in the discipline that seeks to serve the church and change the world. This also means, I am convinced, that the boundaries of analytic theology, the appropriate topics and legitimate areas of inquiry, may need to be stretched and expanded.

Epigraph: Karl Barth, *Church Dogmatics*, vol. I/1, *The Doctrine of the Word of God*, ed. T. F. Torrance, trans. Geoffrey Bromiley (Edinburgh: T & T Clark, 1975), p. 3.
[1]Nicholas Wolterstorff, "To Theologians: From One Who Cares About Theology but Is Not One of You," *Theological Education* (2005): 83.

THE HISTORICAL ADAM AND THE CRISIS OF FAITH: A RECENT CONVERSATION ON CREATION, EVOLUTION AND CHRISTIAN DOCTRINE AS A CASE STUDY

For many centuries, Christians have believed in the truth of the following story. According to this story, God—who is both omnicompetent and omnibenevolent—creates *ex nihilo*. He fashions a universe that is filled with order and purpose, and he calls it *good*. At the height or pinnacle of this creation, he takes material that he has already created, and from this material he forms creatures in his image. These creatures live in a primal state of shalom, and they exercise God-appointed dominion and benevolent care over this primeval paradise. In true righteousness and holiness, they enjoy intimate communion with their Maker and fellowship with each other. But then tragedy strikes—they turn away from him in rebellion. In a word, they *fall*. The results of this sinful rebellion are devastating, and the results have cosmic implications. Humanity now suffers from the effects of this fall, and the results of it produce alienation. The alienation takes no prisoners and leaves nothing untouched: humans are now alienated from God, from one another and indeed from the rest of creation. With this alienation comes suffering and death for humanity. The story continues, of course, for sin never gets the last word in the Christian metanarrative. For the triune God acts—in the election of Israel, ultimately in the incarnation of his own Son and continuously through the Spirit's presence in the church and the world—to redeem his people and indeed to renew all creation.

Not surprisingly, Christians have differed in their understandings of some of the details of the story. But in the main, at least, they have believed in its truth. They have also found it to be very meaningful—they have taken it to make sense of the both the beauty and brokenness of this world as well as their reason for hope. But there is another story, and it is a narrative that many take to be the irreconcilable enemy of the common, traditional Christian story. According to this story, things are radically different. The world was never a place of shalom, and there were no original human persons as depicted in the Genesis story. Humans share a biological and genetic heritage with other hominid species; they are not fundamentally different or unique. Moreover, this genetic and biological legacy has predisposed them to radical selfishness and other proclivities that the Christian tradition has deemed "sinful." And they have had these tendencies from "the beginning." Humans did not come into existence by any special divine action, and they did not—at any time—exist in some primeval state of innocence. Instead, to be clear, they are the product of forces that predetermined them toward "sinful" behaviors. To the extent that we might be able to talk about moral responsibility of the earliest members of our species, it would seem that these "immature, biologically driven, intellectually naive and confused" primates had no chance.[2] There was no act of "original sin" that somehow supposedly threw everything off kilter (at least not in any sense that remotely resembles traditional Christian doctrine). But then this isn't too surprising; after all, if there were no original sinners, then it isn't strange to conclude that there was no original sin.

It isn't at all hard to see the appearance of deep and irreconcilable differences between these stories. Neither are the matters inconsequential; for all their disagreements, many proponents of both sides concur in their belief that these issues really matter. Sometimes the first and traditional story is held on "biblical" grounds, and all those who might demur or disagree are then accused of rejecting nothing less than the Christian faith. On the other hand, the latter, revisionist story claims impressive support from astronomy, physics, geology, paleoanthropology, genetics and evolutionary biology.[3] Indeed, given the scientific support, "nowadays we are informed that no one save the most incurable rubes can give the [traditional] story any credence at all."[4]

A recent theological conversation on this controversial issue offers us a sort of test case. Here we can see how analytic theology might assist in the task of constructive Christian theology that is guided and normed by Scripture, attentive to and respectful of the Christian tradition, and informed by and engaged with human claims to knowledge and meaning. The broad lines of the traditional position are well known, so I shall

---

[2]John R. Schneider, "Recent Genetic Science and Christian Theology on Human Origins: An 'Aesthetic Supralapsarianism,'" *Perspectives on Science and the Christian Faith* (2010): 202.
[3]Hud Hudson offers a concise summary of these claims, *The Fall and Hypertime* (Oxford: Oxford University Press, 2014), pp. 23-29.
[4]Ibid., p. 36.

proceed to a description of what I shall call the revisionist account. Following this, I offer a summary of what I will refer to as a traditionalist response. With this background, we will be in a position to see how analytic theology might be of assistance.

Original sin and original sinners: A revisionist account. Daniel Harlow and John Schneider offer a proposal for dealing with such challenges to traditional Christian doctrine. Since it is representative of much recent work on the topic, it deserves a closer look. They are very familiar with the challenges modern science brings to the traditional Christian doctrine of original sin. As Harlow puts it, "Recent studies in primatology, sociobiology, and phylogenetics [as well as molecular biology] . . . [provide] a range of evidence [that] establishes that virtually all of the acts considered 'sinful' in humans are part of the natural repertoire of behavior among animals . . . behaviors including deception, bullying, theft, rape, murder, infanticide, and warfare" are all very natural.[5] Indeed, "far from infecting the rest of the animal creation with selfish behaviors, we humans inherited these tendencies from our animal past."[6] Moreover, they are sure that contemporary science shows conclusively that human life is homologous with other life—"that is, similar because derived from a common source."[7] Harlow and Schneider take these claims to be established beyond any reasonable doubt. They are also clear about what they see as being at stake in discussion of such matters. On one hand, they know that the claims of modern science seem "to be in conflict with the doctrines comprised by classical Protestant teaching on the historical Fall . . . [doctrines which are] firmly imbedded in major denominational confessions, and . . . are master threads in the logical fabric of Protestant theology as a whole."[8] But they also evince a fundamental commitment to bringing Christianity "up to date" with late modernity for the sake of respectability. Thus Harlow says, "For Christianity to remain intellectually credible and culturally relevant, it must be willing to revise—and thereby enrich—

---

[5]Daniel Harlow, "After Adam: Reading Genesis in an Age of Evolutionary Science," *Perspectives on Science and the Christian Faith* (2010): 180.
[6]Ibid.
[7]Schneider, "Recent Genetic Science," p. 202.
[8]Ibid., p. 196.

its formulation of classic doctrines if the secure findings of science call for revision."[9]

So, facing such challenges to traditional doctrine, what are the options for Christians? Harlow lays out several possibilities: (1) the position known as young-earth creationism holds that Adam and Eve are "recent ancestors"; (2) so-called old-earth creationists suggest that "God created humans around 150,000 years ago but then selected a pair of them about 10,000 years ago to represent all humanity; this would make Adam and Eve *recent representatives*"; (3) others see Adam and Eve as "*ancient ancestors*—a pair of evolved hominids whom God selected and miraculously modified into the first Homo sapiens" or similarly as "*ancient representatives*."[10] These approaches all share in common what Schneider labels "concordism," which he describes as the view that "for any true assertion in science (or for any true assertion at all), no logical conflict *can* exist between it and *any* assertion of Scripture. In other words, it is necessarily true that positive concord exists between all true statements of science and all statements in Scripture, rightly understood—hence the term, 'concordism.'"[11] The Schneider-Harlow proposal rejects "concordism" as inadequate for dealing with the claims of science.[12] In its place, they suggest that we take Adam and Eve as "strictly literary figures—characters in a divinely inspired story about the imagined past that intends to teach primarily theological, not historical, truths about God, creation, and humanity."[13]

What does this proposal yield as a positive doctrinal position on original sin? It yields a position that stoutly opposes the "freewill defense" as an explanation of the fall into original sin. Surely we cannot look at the broken world around us, suffering as it does from the senselessly destructive effects of human sin, and say that the human condition (and the world) in it current state is "not the way its supposed to be."[14] What

---

[9]Harlow, "After Adam," p. 192.

[10]Ibid., p. 181 (emphasis original).

[11]Schneider, "Recent Genetic Science," p. 197 (emphasis original).

[12]Ibid., p. 200.

[13]Harlow, "After Adam," p. 181. Whether or not "concordism" is really inconsistent with viewing Adam and Eve as strictly literary figures is open to question, but Harlow and Schneider assume that it is.

[14]Schneider polemicizes against Plantinga, e.g., "Recent Genetic Science," pp. 208, 211 n. 40.

it does give us is this: a reading of the biblical text that says both that Adam and Eve are strictly literary (*rather than* historical) characters in Genesis and that the assertions of Luke and Paul are simply mistaken. It accepts the insights of sociobiology with gratitude, for here we have independent witness to "the inevitability of human sin and the inability of human beings to overcome their inherited tendency to sin."[15] And it provides a theology that concludes,

> A great many things that people previously believed came about through human sin, did not come about that way. They came through the creative-destructive will of God. The disorder in the world—even grotesque injustice—exists because, in a sense that only poets dare describe, while God does not approve the injustice that exists, God strangely does approve the world in which, as a matter of *fact*, the injustice exists, and in the way of liberating the world, God sometimes mysteriously does cause injustice to occur. In other words, Job has been right all along: it is *God* who slays him, and none other.[16]

Thus we come to an "aesthetic supralapsarianism": *God* made it inevitable that this would be a world of toil, sweat, blood and tears; *God* made sin and misery inevitable, and it has been so since the beginning. But God did this in order that he might bring incarnation and atonement—and that he might be pleased by the beauty of it all when taken together. This world—in both its gory primeval past and its horrific present—is exactly the way that it *is* supposed to be. But it is what it is supposed to be only in a penultimate sense, because it sets things up or arranges the cosmos so that God ultimately "may have mercy on them all."[17] What remains of the doctrine of original sin is the fact (now supported by sociobiology) that harmfully selfish behaviors are intrinsic to humanity. What does not remain are such venerable propositions as these: (1) a historical Adam and Eve existed in God-intended innocence and shalom and then "fell"; (2) their fall has affected all of humanity by infecting our nature with sin; and (3) all of creation has somehow been "thrown off" by this tragedy in Eden.

Their arguments to support this proposal may be seen in several steps.

---

[15]Harlow, "After Adam," p. 191.

[16]Schneider, "Recent Genetic Science," p. 207.

[17]Schneider quotes Rom 11:32, ibid., p. 208.

First, Harlow advances hermeneutical and exegetical arguments to show that Adam and Eve are properly seen in Genesis 2-3 only as "symbolic-literary figures," and to show that "most interpreters do not find the doctrines of the Fall and original sin in the text of Genesis 2-3 but only in later Christian readings of it."[18] He offers reflection on the literary genre of Genesis 1-11; here he discusses "Genesis' reliance on and Refutation of Mesopotamian Myths," and he concludes that "what we have in Genesis is not propositional revelation, but narrative theology."[19] He argues further that the presence in Genesis 1-2 of two creation accounts counts against their historicity; here he concludes that because these accounts have "so many discrepancies, neither of them can be taken to offer factual history."[20] He also makes much of the symbolic and literary elements in Genesis 1-3, and he concludes that when we take Genesis 2-3 "on its own terms," it gets us nowhere near the classical Christian doctrine of original sin.[21]

The next step is to make a case that while Paul and Luke were mistaken about the historicity of Adam, this really does not matter so much because "Paul's main interest is to depict Christ as a representative figure, one whose act affected not only himself but the entire human race," and thus "a historical Adam is not essential to his teaching."[22] So while Jesus indeed *is* a historical figure, and while Paul places him as exactly parallel to Adam (in this and other, though not all respects), this is ancillary to Paul's main point. So to keep the main point that Paul is trying to make, Harlow concludes, one need not retain belief in a historical Adam.

The next step concerns historical theology. Here the advocates of the view recognize that what they are doing is truly revolutionary (at least, they say, in "the West"). As Schneider admits, the force of the tradition is diametrically opposed to his view. "All conservative Protestant denominations have enshrined the historical Fall, officially or unofficially, in their confessions, catechisms, and dogmatic expositions of the faith."[23]

---

[18]Harlow, "After Adam," p. 181.
[19]Ibid., p. 185.
[20]Ibid.
[21]Ibid., pp. 187-88.
[22]Ibid., p. 190.
[23]Schneider, "Recent Genetic Science," p. 200.

The proponents of the revisionist view recognize that their proposal has far-reaching implications that go far beyond the interpretation of a passage of Scripture (or several thereof). Those implications affect the most fundamental Christian beliefs about the dignity and depravity of humanity, and the revisionist view also has serious implications for our understanding of the purposes of God and the work of God incarnate on our behalf.[24] So what does the Harlow-Schneider proposal offer? Their reply goes as follows: While it may be true enough that the majority of the Latin tradition both accepts and relies on the view that Adam was a historical person (who really fell, and whose fall has affected us all), there are elements of the "Eastern tradition" as well as minority reports within Western Christianity that opt for a "supralapsarian" theology. In other words, while much Western (both Protestant and Roman Catholic) theology has assumed that the incarnation of the Son of God was a sort of "plan B" (or "emergency plan"), there are notable theologians within the tradition (Irenaeus and Barth are the two most important for Schneider) who insist that the incarnation was God's original plan all along. In other words, for these theologians the incarnation of the Son was "plan A."[25] The historical-theological payoff of such a claim seems to be this: there is, after all, some support for the revisionist proposal within the tradition (or, more modestly, that there are positions within the tradition in which the new proposal can find hospitable space).

The historical point, however, really only (or mostly) serves to set up the theological one. Schneider notes that while the "doctrine of a historical Fall is not just a master thread in the fabric of western Christian theology . . . this doctrine also provides the crucial metaphysical framework for important versions of Christian theodicy, notably the free will defense."[26] Schneider claims that if God provided humans with freedom so that they might thrive and flourish, then God's plan must be judged to be a failure.[27] So what Schneider really wants—and what he thinks his revisionist proposal gets—is an acceptable theodicy. It is a

---

[24]See Harlow, "After Adam," pp. 191-92.
[25]Schneider, "Recent Genetic Science," p. 203.
[26]Ibid., p. 204.
[27]Ibid., pp. 204-5.

theodicy in which the utter sovereignty of God is witnessed in an unrivaled manner. God is, after all, the agent who makes everything happen in just the way he intends. And it is one that accepts the world—in all of its stench and filth—as the "way it *was* meant to be." Finally, it is one that does not worry so much about moral responsibility as it does about escape from misery. And since this misery has been brought on everyone *by God*, we are, presumably, to be confident that the mercy will also bring escape from misery for all.[28]

Original righteousness and original sinners: A traditionalist response. C. John Collins defends the broadly traditional view critiqued by revisionists such as Harlow, Schneider and others,[29] and he does so with awareness of the complexity of the issues and the strength of the challenges. He is aware of the hermeneutical issues at stake; he knows that "themes in Genesis parallel themes that we find in stories from other ancient Near Eastern cultures"; and he is aware that

> recent advances in biology seem to push us further away from any idea of an original human couple through whom sin and death came into the world. The evolutionary history of mankind shows us that death and struggle have been part of existence on earth from the earliest moments. Most recently, discoveries about the features of human DNA seem to require that the human population has always had at least as many as a thousand members.[30]

Nonetheless, he presses on in defense of the traditional position.

Collins's strategy involves several steps. First, he argues that the broad canonical narrative of biblical theology makes no sense without a historical first couple and a historical "fall." As he puts it, "Any telling of the Biblical story must include the notion of *sin*: human beings are estranged from God."[31] Sin, in the biblical story, is portrayed as "an alien intruder into God's good creation," and the story of Adam and Eve is the Bible's way of describing "how this intruder first came into human experience."[32]

---

[28]Ibid., p. 204.
[29]See also C. John Collins, "A Historical Adam: Old-Earth Creation View," in *Four Views on the Historical Adam*, ed. Matthew Barrett and Ardel Caneday (Grand Rapids: Zondervan Academic, 2013), pp. 143-75.
[30]Ibid.
[31]Ibid., p. 42.
[32]Ibid., p. 49.

So if the "Bible writers portray this as the true story for all people every-where," if the "best way to read the parts of the Bible . . . is in relation to the overarching story," and if this story demands a historical first couple and a historical fall, then Christians have good reason for maintaining belief in the traditional account.[33]

Collins continues by arguing for this conclusion from consideration of specific texts. With respect to the Genesis account itself, he makes a case for literary unity, and he argues that we should take the author of Genesis to be "talking about what he thought were actual events, using rhetorical and literary techniques to shape the readers' attitudes toward those events."[34] He concludes that the Genesis account gives us plenty of reasons to resist an overly literalistic interpretation, but he also argues that the text gives us reasons to "accept an historical core."[35] Collins goes on to support this from other important Old Testament texts and from the literature of Second Temple Judaism as well as the Gospels, the Pauline corpus and other New Testament texts. Appealing especially to the teachings of Jesus on divorce (e.g., Mt 19:4-5) and the death of Abel (Mt 23:35; Lk 11:51; cf. Gen 4:8), he concludes that "it is fair to say that the Gospel writers portray Jesus as someone who believed both that Adam and Eve were actual people, and that their disobedience changed things for us their descendants."[36] Turning to Pauline theology, he surveys several important recent commentators, and he concludes by agreeing with N. T. Wright:

> Paul clearly believed that there had been a single first pair, whose male, Adam, had been given a commandment and had broken it. Paul was, we may be sure, aware of what we would call mythical or metaphorical dimensions to the story, but he would not have regarded these as throwing doubt on the existence, and primal sin, of the first historical pair. Our knowledge of early anthropology is sketchy, to put it mildly. Each time another very early skull is dug up the

---

[33]Ibid.
[34]Ibid., p. 16. He contrasts this way of reading with three alternatives: the author intended to relay "straight" history as if from a modern textbook; the author intended to "recount an imaginary history" by the use of standard literary conventions to express general statements; or the author told a story without any interest or regard for historicity.
[35]Ibid., p. 66.
[36]Ibid., p. 78.

newspapers exclaim over the discovery of the first human beings; we have consigned Adam and Eve entirely to the world of mythology, but we are still looking for their replacements. . . . The general popular belief that the early stories of Genesis were straightforwardly disproved by Charles Darwin is of course nonsense, however many times it is reinforced in contemporary myth-making. Things are just not that simple, in biblical theology or science.[37]

Pulling this biblical evidence together, Collins concludes that it gives us several important criteria. First, we should conclude that the origin "of the human race goes beyond a merely natural process." Second, "we should see Adam and Eve at the headwaters of the race." Third, the "'fall,' in whatever form it took, was both historical (it happened) and moral (it involved disobeying God), and it occurred at the beginning of the human race." Finally, "if someone should decide that there were, in fact, more human beings than just Adam and Eve at the beginning of mankind, then . . . he should envision these humans as a single tribe" with Adam as "the chieftain of this tribe."[38]

So these are, according to Collins, the important theological criteria. But what about the claims of evolutionary biology, paleontology and primatology? Collins is well aware that there are many Christians who wish to hold to these theological criteria; he is also acquainted with Christians who do not wish to dismiss the scientific evidence out of hand. Neither does Collins himself want to dismiss the scientific evidence. So what is the Christian to do? Collins rehearses several possible scenarios. He realizes that some Christians (especially, but not only, young-earth creationists) want to insist that Adam and Eve are the first members of the species *Homo*. The major problem with this should be obvious from the rehearsal of the scientific claims: according to those claims, the earliest *Homo* is dated very long ago and "without any specific cultural remains in the paleontological record."[39] Other approaches allow for the development of other hominid species but see the special creation of the human race as more recent: thus "Adam and Eve are historical indi-

---

[37]Ibid., pp. 87-88, quoting N. T. Wright, "Romans," in *The New Interpreter's Bible*, vol. 10, *Acts, Introduction to Epistolary Literature, Romans, 1 Corinthians*, ed. Leander E. Keck (Nashville: Abingdon, 2002), p. 526.

[38]Ibid., pp. 120-21.

[39]Ibid., p. 122.

viduals—the first human beings—originating by God's miraculous intervention approximately 70,000 to 50,000 years ago," and their "descendants formed a small initial population that eventually gave rise to all
human populations around the world."[40]

Still other approaches allow for the creation of Adam and Eve via the
refurbishment and enhancement of hominids that are already in existence. For instance, the "evolutionary creationist" Gavin McGrath suggests that God may have taken two preexisting hominids, reformed one
(Adam) in the divine image and then took the other (Eve) and used
genetic material from the first (from his "rib") to remake her. According
to this suggestion, "these two *alone* are the rest of the human race's
progenitors."[41] Other scholars, alert to the fact that Genesis 4 seems to
indicate the presence of other humans, suggest that God retools a group
of preexisting hominids and appoints the first human pair as "vice regents" and thus makes Adam the "federal head" whose representative
work spreads "outwards to his contemporaries as well as onwards to his
offspring."[42] Collins is far from dogmatic in recommendation at this
point, but he does think there is value in seeing how various approaches
might be (or, with some tweaking, might become) consistent with the
theological criteria derived from Scripture. "Nothing," he says, "requires
us to abandon monogenesis altogether for some form of polygenesis;
rather, a modified monogenesis, which keeps Adam and Eve, can do the
job."[43] So while he admits that there is much that is uncertain in the
work of putting together a full-orbed Christian view of these matters, he
also insists that these remaining uncertainties "in no way undermine our
right to hold fast to the Biblical story line with full confidence."[44]

Peter Enns is not persuaded by such maneuvers. Such strategies for
reconciling the teaching of Scripture and the claims of science, he says,

---

[40]Ibid., p. 123, quoting Fazale Rana with Hugh Ross, *Who Was Adam? A Creation Model Approach to the Origin of Man* (Colorado Springs: NavPress, 2005), p. 248.

[41]Collins, *Did Adam and Eve*, p. 123, quoting from Gavin Basil McGrath, "Soteriology: Adam and the Fall," *Perspectives on Science and Christian Faith* (1997): 263.

[42]Collins, *Did Adam and Eve*, p. 124, quoting Derek Kidner, *Genesis*, Tyndale Old Testament Commentary (Downers Grove, IL: InterVarsity Press, 1967), p. 29.

[43]Collins, *Did Adam and Eve*, p. 130.

[44]Ibid., p. 131.

leave us "with a first pair that is utterly foreign to the biblical portrait."[45] Enns objects to the suggestion that "Adam and Eve were two hominids or symbolic of a group of hominids with whom, at some point in evolutionary development, God entered into a relationship" and "endowed them with his image."[46] Taking the Bible to teach a "sudden and recent" creation of humanity, he rejects these proposed scenarios as "alternate and wholly ad hoc"—and finally not "biblical."[47] Thus he concludes that "scientific and biblical models of human origins are, strictly speaking, incompatible.... They cannot be reconciled, and there is no 'Adam' to be found in an evolutionary scheme."[48]

Toward clarity: Analytic theology between biblical studies and science. What are we to make of such debates? *How* are we to make sense of such debates? How should we evaluate them? Hud Hudson argues that analytic theology "deserves a clearly marked place at this conversational table," for "metaphysical and epistemological tools and insights are often at the core of our abilities to make scientific progress, to interpret religious texts and traditions, and to combine these unique perspectives on the world into a unified and intelligible whole."[49] Indeed, "the health and success of the dialogue between science and religion are endangered by not attending properly to the philosophical presuppositions and philosophical restrictions that are operative in the relevant debates."[50] So *how* might analytic theology be of assistance in these debates? One way an analytic approach might help is simply by clarifying some important but oft-confused issues and terms. For instance, consider the "self-evident problem" that Peter Enns raises: "Evolution demands that the special creation of the first Adam as described in the Bible is not literally historical; however, Paul seems to require it.... If evolution is true, then Christianity is false."[51] He recognizes that "the issue is not whether science and religion in general can be reconciled." No, the "issue before

---

[45]Enns, *The Evolution of Adam*, p. xvii.
[46]Ibid., p. 138.
[47]Ibid., p. 139.
[48]Ibid., p. 138.
[49]Hudson, *Fall and Hypertime*, p. 1.
[50]Ibid., pp. 10-11.
[51]Enns, *Evolution of Adam*, p. xvi.

us is more pressing: can evolution and a biblically rooted Christian faith coexist?"[52] So "deep Christian commitments lead one to read Paul and Genesis with utmost seriousness, but scientific sensibilities do not allow one to dismiss evolution."[53] In response to this "dilemma," Enns sees four options. One is simply to "accept evolution and reject Christianity." Another option, at the opposite end, is simply to "accept Paul's view of Adam as binding and reject evolution." A slightly better option is to "reconcile evolution and Christianity by positing a first human pair (or group) at some point in the evolutionary process," but Enns, as we saw, rejects this option in favor of a fourth: "rethink Genesis and Paul." By "rethink" Enns means that we should think that Paul believed in a historical Adam—*and* that we should think Paul was wrong. Notice that Enns repeatedly uses the term *evolution* as if the precise meaning is somehow self-evident or obvious. He thinks that "evolution" is a "game-changer," because it

> tells us that human beings are not the product of a special creative act by God as the Bible says but are the end product of a process of trial-and-error adaptation and natural selection. This process began billions of years ago, with the simplest of one-cell life forms, and developed into the vast array of life on this planet—plants, reptiles, fish, mammals, and so forth—with humanity. These humans also happen to share a close common ancestry with primates.[54]

But the meaning of the beguiling term *evolution* is not so self-evident or obvious. To the contrary, it can harbor many different meanings. The term *evolution* might carry any of the following meanings:[55]

E1 The earth is very old (and life forms have developed and changed).

E2 Life has progressed from relatively simple to very complex forms.

E3 *Descent with modification.*

E4 *Common ancestry.*

E5 *Naturalistic mechanism* (e.g., "natural selection" combined with random

[52]Ibid.
[53]Ibid., p. xvii.
[54]Ibid., p. xiv.
[55]My debt to Alvin Plantinga's work will be obvious, e.g., Alvin Plantinga, *Where the Conflict Really Lies: Science, Religion, and Naturalism* (Oxford: Oxford University Press, 2011), pp. 8-9.

genetic mutation), according to which the species *Homo sapiens* has evolved from other primitive hominid primates through a long, cruel and bloody process marked by selfishness, death and genocide.

E6 *Naturalist origins.*

Note how many of these—explicitly, E1, E2, E3, E4 and E5—are included in Enns's summary. But they are included without being properly distinguished. Despite the fact that they are sometimes treated as a kind of "package deal" (as Enns appears to treat them), there are important conceptual differences here. The claims of, say, E1 and E2 are a long way off from, say, E5. Neither does scientific evidence for one obviously count as evidence for another; evidence that the earth is very old count does not count as evidence for the common-ancestry thesis. Belief in, say, E5 is not entailed by commitment to E1 or acceptance of, say, E3. Different lines of evidence, and evidence of varying levels of strength, are adduced in support of these theses. But not all the evidence that supports one (or more) of these theses can be taken seriously as support for others.

If my point about the legitimacy and importance of these distinctions isn't clear, consider E6. Clearly, E6 is inconsistent with traditional Christian doctrine. But E6 is also a distinctly *metaphysical* thesis. I do not think it is a scientific thesis at all. Or, if it is, then at the least it is not merely or only a scientific thesis; if it is a scientific thesis at all, then it is a science-plus-metaphysics thesis. Surely it is true that E6 can claim widespread and enthusiastic support, and it is no less true that E6 can claim this widespread and enthusiastic support *among scientists*. But none of this changes the fact that it is a metaphysical thesis. As a metaphysical thesis, any evidential support from the natural sciences that can be adduced in favor of the other theses doesn't amount to proof of E6 or evidence for it. How does geological evidence for a very old earth support an argument for the conclusion that God does not exist? How does genetic and biological evidence for the conclusion that humans share a common ancestry with other primates support metaphysical naturalism? Such attempts at argument, however enthusiastically stated by the "New Atheists," are simply non sequiturs. It is also worth pointing out that E6 is a metaphysical thesis with deep flaws.[56] But the main point should be clear: there are oft-overlooked but important distinctions here, and we would do well to proceed with care.

Similarly, *creation* might mean any of the following (or more) in contemporary theological (and apologetics) discourse:

C1 The cosmos was created by an uncreated Creator.

C2 The universe was created *ex nihilo* and was originally and primordially *good*.

C3 Humans are created *imago Dei*.

C4 A first human pair (by name: "Adam and Eve") were created specially by God.

C5 The creation bears intelligible marks of "fine-tuning" and/or "intelligent design."

C6 The earth is very "young" (ca. six thousand to ten thousand years old), and was created in six twenty-four-hour periods.

Again, as with the term *evolution*, there are some very important distinctions here. And, when pressed into service, they will do some important work for us.

Two steps back: Analyzing the debate. Note first how Harlow and Schneider portray "evolutionary science."[57] Harlow says that "modern science has amply demonstrated that phenomena such as predation, death, and the extinction of species have been intrinsic and even necessary aspects of life on earth for billions of years, long before the arrival of *Homo sapiens*."[58] He also says that "the ever-growing hominid fossil record unmistakably shows that human beings did not appear suddenly but evolved gradually over the course of six million years," and he says further that recent "research in molecular biology indicates that the genetic diversity of the present human population cannot possibly be

---

[56]Plantinga's famous "evolutionary argument against naturalism" is important here, e.g., *Warranted Christian Belief* (Oxford: Oxford University Press, 2000), pp. 199-240; and *Where the Conflict Really Lies*, pp. 307-50. See also Michael C. Rea's *World Without Design: The Ontological Consequences of Naturalism* (Oxford: Oxford University Press, 2004).

[57]Repeatedly, this is Schneider's term, e.g., "Recent Genetic Science," pp. 196, 197, 204, 205.

[58]Harlow, "After Adam," p. 179.

traced back to a single couple living in Mesopotamia a few thousand years ago."[59] Instead, the "ancestors of all modern *Homo sapiens* were a population of about 10,000 interbreeding individuals who were members of a much larger population living in Africa around 150,000 years ago."[60] This is, he concludes, what we get from "evolutionary science."[61] Notice what is included together: explicit avowal of E1, E3, E4 and E5 (with E2 likely assumed). Note as well that these are all lumped together. E4 seems confused with E5, and the evidence for E4 seems to be taken as support for E5. But E4 and E5 are distinct, and evidence that all living creatures are related to one another and stem from a common source is not evidence that evolution has occurred by some particular process. Similarly, evidence that humans are closely related to other hominid species is not evidence that there was no direct (and perhaps miraculous) divine involvement. As with Enns, so also with Harlow and Schneider: these distinctions are overlooked, and these different meanings of *evolution* are not adequately distinguished. Consequently, it becomes very hard to know exactly which strands of scientific evidence support exactly which conclusions.

Turning to Harlow's interpretation of biblical teaching, I think we can see that he makes some valid and very helpful observations about the text (within its historical context). He makes some good points about literary genre (especially in Gen 1–3); there are important issues here that are all too often missed or overlooked by people on various sides of these issues (not least by scientists). He is right to observe both the parallels and the sharp and crucial contrasts between the Genesis account and the various parallel myths from the ancient Near East. Perhaps most helpfully, he highlights some critical theological differences between Genesis and parallel accounts of origins. Furthermore, he is right to caution against reading too much into the Genesis account when taken alone. Moreover, he helps us see the significant symbolic elements in the text.

But none of this leads us to Harlow's conclusion that Adam and Eve were merely literary creations (rather than actual, historical persons). None of his points, whether taken individually or collectively, either says

---

[59]Ibid., pp. 179-80.
[60]Ibid., p. 180.
[61]Ibid., p. 181.

or implies that Adam and Eve did not actually exist but were only literary creations. Harlow is right to observe literary conventions and symbols in the account, and he is right to see that Genesis 1–3 is not some kind of disinterested historical account. Indeed, the theological points made in Genesis come via the polemical use of the symbolism. But to recognize all this does not in any way entail that Adam and Eve were *not* historical characters. It would if an argument such as the following were sound:

(1) If there are parallels with other ancient Near Eastern literature, literary conventions or symbolic elements present within the text, then the main characters either could not have been or very probably were not historical persons.

(2) There are parallels with other ancient Near Eastern literature, literary conventions and symbolic elements present in the Genesis account;

(3) Therefore, the main characters in the Genesis account either could not have been or very probably were not historical persons.

If such an argument were sound, then Harlow would be on solid ground, for he has established good grounds for accepting point 2. But this argument *isn't* a good argument—for it suffers from the defect of having a first premise that is manifestly untrue. Or, more modestly, point 1 is not *obviously* true, and Harlow gives us no argument (good or otherwise) for thinking it is true. He gives us some salutary cautions about reading the text with hermeneutical sophistication and exegetical sensitivity. And for this we can be grateful. But so far as I can see, this does not give us a compelling reason to think that Adam and Eve were not historical figures.

Such an argument is so bad that we should assume Harlow does not intend it. So maybe Harlow doesn't mean that his case implies that Adam and Eve were not historical persons; perhaps he only means that his view opens the door to such a conclusion. Fair enough. But then such an argument clearly does not support the conclusion that Adam and Eve were not historical persons. At most it leaves the question unresolved and opens the door to consideration of other evidence. But what do we find when we look at other evidence? Well, when we look at the further evidence from Scripture, it becomes clear—as Harlow recognizes—that the overall biblical account really does teach a historical Adam. After all, even Harlow admits that Paul teaches this—and Pauline theology is rather important for a canonical account. Even if it turns out that Harlow is right that our grounds for believing in the historicity of Adam and Eve are somehow undermined by the parallels and use of literary devices, even if he is right that from Genesis alone (when properly interpreted with historical-critical methodology) we don't have reason to believe that Adam and Eve were historical people, this still doesn't give us reason to reject the conclusion that Adam and Eve were historical figures. After all, as Christian readers of the Bible, we do not have "Genesis alone." Paul, for instance, offers an important interpretation of the Genesis passage, and he makes obvious his conclusion: as Jesus Christ is a historical person whose presence and work have changed the world, so also is Adam.

Harlow concludes that "what we have in Genesis is not propositional revelation but narrative theology."[62] But he gives us no reason to think that these are mutually exclusive options. The real issue is not, it seems to me, whether we are dealing with "propositions." The real issue is whether we are dealing with revelation. A theological claim may well be couched in narrative; indeed, in much of Scripture this is exactly what we have. But if it is theological at all, then surely it is a claim about God (or God and the world, or the world as created by God, or sinners in relation to God, etc.). Harlow himself describes the gods of the ancient Near Eastern accounts as "capricious and immoral," while God in Genesis should be seen "by contrast" to these deities of the pagan world.[63] I concur with Harlow that there are important theological claims being made, and that there is a direct and powerful contrast. But consider:

P By contrast to the gods of the ancient Near East, Yahweh is not capricious or immoral.

What kind of a claim is *P*? Once we recognize that a "proposition is an abstraction that captures or expresses the descriptive content of a complete statement," it is easy indeed to see that *P* expresses a proposi-

---

[62]Ibid., p. 185.
[63]Ibid., pp. 183-84.

tional claim (one that could be translated into sentences in other languages).[64] It may be communicated via "narrative theology," but it is a propositional claim nonetheless. Being clear on just what a proposition (which is commonly the work, incidentally, of the analytic crowd) actually *is* helps us see that—on Harlow's own account—the "narrative theology" of the opening chapters of Genesis does intend to convey propositional truth claims. Of course it is true that this narrative theology might do a lot more than make such truth claims; it has the ability to do many things with words, and it would be both mistaken and unhelpful to "flatten" Genesis into the mold of "modern" historiography (or, worse yet, to interpret it as if it were intended as a modern science textbook). Theology is not only or merely about making propositional claims. But if narrative theology really is theology, then it is making some propositional claims about God (regardless of how it communicates these claims). So when Harlow says that this is narrative theology and *not* propositional revelation, we can dismiss the red herring about "propositions."

Schneider appeals to "Eastern" theology and to the "supralapsarian" views of some "Western" theologians. His references to Eastern theology fail to cite (or even name) those who would actually support his proposal, but he does mention Irenaeus as a theologian who was a "supralapsarian." In other words, Irenaeus was a proponent of the view that the incarnation was part of the original divine plan (rather than "an inferior 'Plan B'").[65] He mentions Irenaeus several times, but he does not offer any real exposition of Irenaeus's theology. The fact that Schneider does not lay out, explain or defend Irenaeus's own views does not stop him, however, from concluding that we cannot hold that the traditional view tells us of "how things really were in the primal human past" for "sound Irenaean reasons of theology."[66]

Schneider is right that there is a "supralapsarian" Christology in the broad Christian tradition. This theology is there for good reason; there

---

[64]David K. Clark, *To Know and Love God: Method in Theology* (Wheaton, IL: Crossway, 2003), p. 358.
[65]Schneider, "Recent Genetic Science," p. 203.
[66]Ibid.

is a sense in which Jesus Christ is "the Lamb who was slain from the creation of the world" (Rev 13:8), and the earliest apostolic proclamation makes it clear that the incarnation, crucifixion and resurrection of Jesus happened "by God's deliberate plan and foreknowledge" (Acts 2:23; cf. Acts 4:28). But Schneider claims a lot more than this, and he draws some far-reaching conclusions from this supralapsarian Christology. This is where things start to get rather sketchy, and these further claims are open to criticism. It is one thing to point out, as Schneider does, that the incarnation of the Son was not a kind of frantic response to an unforeseen emergency. It is another thing entirely, however, to move from the observation that the Son would have become incarnate regardless of human action to the conclusions that there was no "fall" or that the sinful world is just as God intended it. In other words, the central affirmation of supralapsarian Christology—"incarnation anyway"—does not at all entail "incarnation *and sin* anyway." It is another thing yet to insist that all the sin and misery in the world is somehow *necessary*. Whether or not it is right to affirm "incarnation and sin anyway" on other grounds, it is misleading to present Irenaeus and other theologians (of some vague "Eastern" tradition) as if they also affirmed such a view. In sum, when Schneider claims that there is an element of supralapsarian theology within the tradition, he is almost certainly correct.[67] But when he goes on to appeal to the historic affirmations of supralapsarianism as somehow supportive of his own proposal, he is almost certainly mistaken.

Moving beyond the historical-theological issues to those of dogmatic importance, however, larger questions loom. On one such version of the revisionist proposal, Daryl Domning concludes that the terrible injustices and terrible sufferings of humanity are "just inherent in the existence of a physical and moral universe."[68] Domning's conclusion causes Schneider to point out that on such a view these horrors are then "inevitable, even for God."[69] Schneider does not wrestle with the theological questions raised by such claims, but it is important to take note of them.

---

[67]E.g., Edwin Chr. van Driel, *Incarnation Anyway: Arguments for Supralapsarian Christology* (Oxford: Oxford University Press, 2008).

[68]Daryl Domning, with foreword and commentary by Monica K. Hellwig, *Original Selfishness: Original Sin and Evil in Light of Evolution* (Aldershot, UK: Ashgate, 2006), p. 169.

[69]Schneider, "Recent Genetic Science," p. 205.

For if Domning is correct, then is it also true that suffering and death just *are* essential aspects of what it means to be part of creation? If so, then how is this importantly different from the very gnosticism Irenaeus opposed so strenuously? Traditionally, Christians have insisted on the goodness of creation, and they have likewise insisted that sin is *contra naturem*.[70] The revisionist account holds that this world—in both its gory primeval past and its horrific present—is exactly the way it was supposed to be. Indeed, for such advocates as Domning, this is the way that it *must be*. And here the problems get even worse, for if these horrors are "inevitable, even for God" (and thus are, strictly speaking, necessary), then we are indeed close to both fatalism and gnosticism. Going deeper, we have to wonder: what can we still believe about the goodness of the Creator? Schneider insists that "a great many things that people previously thought came about through human sin, did not come about that way"—instead they came about by the "creative-destructive will of God."[71] But if this is true, then how is sin possibly *contra Deum*? And what might it mean to affirm the goodness of God?

One (half-)step forward: Analysis and the hope for progress. So far, we can see how analytic theology can help us gain clarity on the basic issues involved; the work of careful analysis can assist us in sorting through various (and sometimes inconsistent) meanings of familiar terms. Analytic theology can also help us understand the arguments for and against various proposals, to weigh the evidence for and against those proposals and to evaluate them accordingly. Additionally analytic theology can also press for further clarity regarding the implications— supposed or genuine—of the various proposals.

So where does this leave us? Consider how the various senses of "creation" relate to the various meanings of claims about "evolution." As I observed earlier, E6 is clearly at odds with traditional Christian belief and indeed with theism in general. But as I also pointed out, E6 is a metaphysical doctrine rather than a strictly scientific thesis. Evidence from science does not get us to the metaphysical conclusion; neither,

---

[70]On this theme see Josef Pieper, *The Concept of Sin* (South Bend, IN: St. Augustine's Press, 2001), pp. 34-55.
[71]Schneider, "Recent Genetic Science," p. 207.

apart from a common but unfortunate confusion of physics with metaphysics, is there reason to think that it might. Moreover, E6 is a flawed thesis, and Christians should reject it without blushing. So with that out of the way (for our purposes), consider C1. The thesis that the cosmos was created by an uncreated Creator should not be so much as controversial for Christians (or many other theists). Neither is it at all inconsistent with E1, E2, E3, E4 or E5. Nor yet is there any good reason to think that some evidence adduced from the natural sciences might count against it. I take the situation to be much the same with respect to C2. So far as I can see, there is nothing in C2 that must be incompatible with the claims of E1, for nothing about the thesis that God created *ex nihilo* and to express and share his own goodness is inconsistent with the thesis that the earth is a very old place where life forms have developed and changed over the ages. Similarly with respect to E2, E3 and E4; there is nothing about progression from relatively simple to more complex life forms that rules out an initial creation out of nothing. E5 is more troubling for the conviction expressed in C2 about the goodness of creation. For if the species *Homo sapiens* has evolved from other primate species through a long, cruel and bloody process marked by selfishness, death and genocide *as originally designed by God*, then this might appear to call into question the very goodness of creation. It would be reckless simply to assume that it is consistent with Christian doctrine. It would also, however, be premature to assume that E5 cannot be rendered consistent with the conviction about the goodness of creation expressed in C2. But Christians who want to make peace with E5 will need to think long and hard about this.[72]

Turning our attention from C2 to C3 and C4, again we can see the possibility of concord between these claims and E1, E2 and E3. For again, there is nothing about the conviction that Adam and Eve were created by God in the divine image that is obviously inconsistent with a very old earth, progression from simplicity to complexity or descent with modification. But the "common ancestry" claims of E4, along with the further

---

[72]For some very insightful and helpful suggestions along these lines, see Michael Murray, *Nature Red in Tooth and Claw: Theism and the Problem of Animal Suffering* (Oxford: Oxford University Press, 2008).

detail of how this process works that is provided by E5, indeed do bring us to the appearance of conflict with C4. As we have seen, revisionists such as Enns say that "scientific and biblical models of human origins are, strictly speaking, incompatible. . . . They cannot be reconciled, and there is no 'Adam' to be found in an evolutionary scheme."[73] Similarly, such defenders of the traditional position as Collins recognize the same challenges.[74]

The criticisms of Harlow, Schneider and Enns, while surely motivated by an entirely commendable desire to bring theology into appropriate conversation with the natural sciences, do not show that it is not possible to reconcile belief in a historical Adam and Eve with the claims of the thesis that we share some lineage of common descent. Suppose we take Scripture to teach that the creation of the first humans in the image of God was by special divine action, and that they are uniquely different from the rest of creation by virtue of being in the image of God. But being created by special divine action does not entail that the creation of humanity was *ex nihilo*. On the contrary, the creation of humankind is from preexisting material (the "dust of the ground"). Perhaps, as some reconcilers suggest, God furbished or refurbished an existing pair of hominids and specially endowed them. Perhaps he created genuinely new creatures who have much in common (genetically and biologically) with other hominids—but that also have the divine image. Perhaps they served as "federal representatives" for all humans. With the right (or "wrong") moves in metaphysics, there are various ways to reconcile C4 with not only E1-E3 but also with E4 and E5. From what we do know and don't know, it doesn't seem at all wise to curtail possibilities. And if any of these possibilities is open, then Enns is pretty clearly wrong when he claims that there "cannot" be reconciliation between biblical and scientific claims.

Hud Hudson makes an interesting case for the reconciliation of modern evolutionary theory (roughly, all of what I have called E1-E5) and what he labels "extreme literalism" (which would, I think, include commitment to C1-C4 on the basis of biblical teaching). He is convinced that the "conflict" between the claims of science and the dogmas of the-

---

[73]Enns, *Evolution of Adam*, p. 138.
[74]Collins, *Did Adam and Eve*, p. 12.

ology is not really one of "science" versus "theology" at all; in truth it is science-plus-metaphysics against theology(-with-metaphysical-commitments). With the wrong metaphysics tied to the scientific claims, there indeed is the appearance of conflict. So we need to see and acknowledge the presence of those metaphysical commitments. On the other hand, with the right moves in metaphysics, Hudson concludes that it is possible both to hold to "unabashed, extreme literalism" (which Hudson himself very clearly does *not* hold) about the fall and the doctrine of original sin and to remain "thoroughly consistent with the reigning scientific orthodoxy and the current deliverances of astronomy, physics, geology, paleoanthropology, genetics, and evolutionary biology."[75] The details of Hudson's ingenious approach are complex, and the metaphysics are very controversial, but the basic point should be clear: various strategies are available, and it is misguided—as well as just flat-out mistaken—to proceed as if the contemporary scientific evidence for evolution rules out traditional theological doctrine.

At any rate, with or without Hudson's metaphysics of hypertime, there *are* possibilities. These possibilities might include the sorts of "scenarios" described by Collins. As we have seen, critics such as Enns are not happy with such maneuvers. As he says, such strategies are "utterly foreign to the biblical portrait," "wholly ad hoc" and not finally "biblical."[76] Similarly, Harlow complains that these efforts "read into the biblical text anachronistic notions that would have been inconceivable to the ancient author(s)."[77] Enns even goes so far as to say that the Scripture and science "cannot be reconciled."[78] Note the strength of Enns's claim: he says that Scripture and science *cannot* be reconciled.

But what does it mean to say that some view is "biblical"? And what does it mean to castigate some view as "unbiblical"? Here—as often elsewhere in such debates—it seems to me that charges that some proposition *P* isn't biblical often fly too fast. Recall our earlier discussion of the distinctions between some proposition *P* being *demanded by Scripture,*

---

[75]Hudson, *Fall and Hypertime*, pp. 12-13.
[76]Enns, *Evolution of Adam*, pp. xvii, 139.
[77]Harlow, "After Adam," p. 181.
[78]Enns, *Evolution of Adam*, p. 138.

consistent with Scripture or *inconsistent with Scripture* and our somewhat more finely tuned distinctions between RA1 through RA7 (see chap. 2). Maybe when Enns is arguing that the strategies for reconciling a historical Adam and Eve with the evidence adduced from genetics, biology, primatology and paleontology are "unbiblical," he means that they fail in the sense that they qualify for something like RA6 or RA7. Maybe he is saying that Scripture is *inconsistent with* those strategies; in other words, it is not possible that Scripture be true and any of those scenarios turn out to be true as well. If so, then he has work to do, for he has done nothing to support such a conclusion. Perhaps he only means that these strategies are "unbiblical" in the sense of something more like RA4 or RA5; maybe he merely means to say that these strategies are consistent with Scripture but are not demanded by it. If so, then the defender of these strategies can nod in agreement but then move merrily along. For the defender doesn't need to conclude that the reconciling strategies themselves are demanded by either Scripture or science. To the contrary, so long as both the theological criteria and the scientific desiderata are accounted for, there is no reason to think that "the Bible is opposed to science" or that "scientific and biblical models of human origins are, strictly speaking, incompatible."[79] Accordingly, we can conclude that Enns's claim that "scientific and biblical" accounts of human origins "cannot be reconciled" is far too hasty.

So C5 seems consistent with all of E1-E5. But the challenges reappear when we come to C6. Many Christians believe that the creation is very "recent" or "young"; they are convinced that the Bible clearly teaches (in the sense of RA1 or RA2) that the earth was created in six twenty-four-hour periods only six thousand to ten thousand years ago. Even at first glance, it seems obvious that this position clashes sharply with all the claims of "evolution." But what we would have here would not be "science versus religion" or "theology versus biology" or "creation versus evolution." Instead, what we would have here would be a particular version of the Christian doctrine of creation against a set of claims made and endorsed by many scientists.

---

[79]Ibid.

Surely there is more work remaining on these issues; indeed, it is safe to say that the work is only really beginning. (This case study analyzes only one conversation on only part of the range of issues.) And while analytic theology surely cannot do all the needed work (it should listen to the scientists on the science and the biblical scholars on the exegesis), it should be involved in the collaborative work that is needed if constructive theology is to be done in this area. I suggest that future work should allow eschatology to shed light on protology. It seems to me that theologically based claims about Adam and Eve are parallel to claims about, say, the resurrection in some important ways. We are often reminded that belief in, say, C4 is not "supported" by molecular biology, primatology, sociobiology, phylogenetics and other disciplines in the natural sciences. We are also often reminded that belief in C4 is at odds with metaphysical naturalism (E6). Surely this is all true, but how this counts *against* belief in a historical Adam and Eve is far from obvious. Belief in resurrection isn't "supported" by molecular biology (etc.) either, and it is just as surely at odds with naturalism. Nonetheless, Christians rightly think that they have good grounds for belief in the resurrection of Jesus, and his claims give us good reason to believe in our own resurrection. Christian eschatological belief isn't based on what we learn from the natural sciences, but it is warranted nonetheless.

Shouldn't Christian protological belief enjoy similar epistemic status? If we have reason to believe that, say, Jesus and Paul might have known what they were talking about and were trustworthy, then why shouldn't we take their testimony about protology just as we do about eschatology? An objector might say that the situations are different; in the eschatological case we lack support from the natural sciences but the natural sciences do not contradict resurrection belief, where in the protological case we in fact do have evidence from the natural sciences that contradicts C4. But such an objection doesn't seem weighty at all; to the contrary, it seems just plain wrong. For we *don't* have good evidence from the natural sciences that God *didn't* refurbish existing hominids or create a first human couple that shares strong genetic and biological connections with other primitive hominids. Neither do we have any scientific evidence that God didn't appoint them as representatives. There is no *scientific* evidence against these claims, and we are tempted to think so only if we confuse science with metaphysics. As Hudson says, "The argument from our modern worldview" to the denial of these Christian commitments is "inadequate: it misrepresents itself as a contest between religion and empirical science (a contest we are all too often to regard as akin to a match between a toddler and an 800-pound gorilla), when in fact it requires supplementation by way of a piece of metaphysics that has not been adequately defended or even acknowledged."[80]

Conclusion. As a case study, we have looked at a recent conversation on an important and controversial issue. Through it, we are able to see how analytic theology might help in the task of constructive Christian theology that is engaged with general claims to knowledge in an area of keen interest to Christians. Several points emerge. First, we have seen how analytic theology can help us gain clarity about exactly what we are talking about. Second, it can help us understand the arguments, weigh the evidence for their premises and evaluate them accordingly. Furthermore, it can help us see just what is and what isn't implied or entailed by various arguments or conclusions. Beyond this, analytic theology can help us see where metaphysical (and epistemological) issues are relevant, and it can help us evaluate the metaphysics involved in the various proposals. Finally, it may be that analytic theology can help us make genuine progress. In all these ways, and perhaps many more, analytic theology can be of assistance to constructive Christian theology that seeks genuine and honest engagement with the world.

UNFINISHED BUSINESS: TOWARD BROADER HORIZONS IN ANALYTIC THEOLOGY

To this point, a great deal of analytic philosophy of religion and Christian analytic theology has been focused on a fairly narrow, and sometimes rather predictable, range of topics and issues. For instance, many gallons of ink have been spilled on questions about God's relation to time and eternity. Some philosophers and theologians have argued that God must be, strictly speaking, temporally located rather than timeless. They have

---

[80]Hud Hudson, "An Essay on Eden," *Faith and Philosophy* (2010): 277.

advanced a wide range of arguments in favor of their view; other philosophers and theologians have countered by defending the "traditional" view that God is "atemporal" or somehow "outside" time. Other scholars, meanwhile, have made historical arguments that neither "side" gets the traditional view correct. Similarly, many trees have been the innocent victims of debates about the doctrine of divine simplicity. Again, both philosophers and theologians criticize "the traditional doctrine" on various grounds. And, again, other analytic theologians try both to correct the common contemporary misunderstandings of the tradition and to defend the doctrine against contemporary criticisms. Debates over divine omniscience and creaturely freedom have drawn a great deal of attention, and these show no signs of abatement. The situation is similar with respect to discussions of divine sovereignty and providence (especially with respect to the problems of evil), the doctrines of the Trinity and incarnation, the mind-body debate in theological anthropology and eschatology (especially concerning heaven, hell and purgatory). The same could be said about other issues, especially those related to divine attributes and divine action.

Much of this work is exemplary with respect to clarity, argumentative rigor and other virtues of the analytic tradition. Indeed, some of it is simply stellar. This is not to say that consensus has been reached or that all of the important work is done on the main topics, but it is safe to say that some progress has been made. There is more to do on the central issues of discussion to this point, and I do not mean to discourage these further conversations at all. But these are not the only worthy topics. Nor is it obvious that they are the most worthy topics. To the contrary, there are many other interesting and important issues in Christian doctrine, and many of these would benefit from close and rigorous theological analysis. For instance, consider the underdeveloped areas of inquiry in ecclesiology.[81] *What* is the church? Is it best understood as a four-dimensional entity? What is the relation of the "one" to the "many" in ecclesiology? What happens in the liturgy? What do we learn from the liturgy about

---

[81]See the steps made by William J. Abraham, "Church," in *The Cambridge Companion to Christian Philosophical Theology*, ed. Charles Taliaferro and Chad Meister (Cambridge: Cambridge University Press, 2010), pp. 170-82.

God, Christ, sin and salvation?[82] How should we understand the
sacraments?[83] What is the mission of the church? What happens in acts
of ministry? These questions, and many more, largely await further exploration and analysis.

And moving beyond traditional Christian doctrine per se, the field
becomes even more expansive and inviting. To put it plainly, in addition
to such important work on the well-worn subjects, we need more work
in analytic *political* theology and analytic *moral* theology. There are some
notable exceptions, of course, but a great deal of what takes place in
analytic theology is at some distance from pressing issues in political
theology and moral theology.[84] Meanwhile, some of the discussions in
public and political theology—as well as moral theology—could use a
healthy dose of the clarity, parsimony of expression and (especially) rigor
of argument that are the hallmarks of the analytic tradition.

UNSTARTED BUSINESS: TOWARD A GLOBAL
ANALYTIC THEOLOGY

Up till now I have suggested that analytic theology might usefully extend
into areas that to this point are underexplored and underdeveloped. But
not only is there "unfinished business" in analytic theology, but there are
also vast areas of theology where analytic theology has not even yet really
started to go to work. There are important issues that deserve and need—
even urgently—very careful theological analysis. I refer to the burgeoning enterprise that is sometimes called "global Christian theology."
Timothy Tennent says that "we are living in one of the dramatic shifts in

---

[82]See Nicholas Wolterstorff, *The God We Worship: An Essay in Liturgical Theology* (Grand Rapids: Eerdmans, 2015).

[83]For recent work, see Alexander Pruss, "The Eucharist: Real Presence and Real Absence," in *The Oxford Handbook of Philosophical Theology*, ed. Thomas P. Flint and Michael C. Rea (Oxford: Oxford University Press, 2009), pp. 512-37; and James Arcadi, "Impanation, Incarnation, and Enabling Externalism," *Religious Studies* (2015): 1-16; Arcadi, "A Theory of Consecration: A Philosophical Exposition of a Biblical Phenomenon," *Heythrop Journal* (2013): 913-25. For recent work on the important historical background, see Marilyn McCord Adams, *Some Later Medieval Theories of the Eucharist: Thomas Aquinas, Gilles of Rome, Duns Scotus, and William Ockham* (Oxford: Oxford University Press, 2012).

[84]The work of Christian Miller is an especially bright spot, e.g., *Moral Character: An Empirical Theory* (Oxford: Oxford University Press, 2013); Miller, *Character and Moral Psychology* (Oxford: Oxford University Press, 2014).

Christianity since the Reformation. Christianity is on the move and is creating a seismic change that is changing the face of the whole Christian movement."[85] He observes that "every Christian in the world, but especially those in the West, must understand how these changes will influence . . . our study of theology."[86] Tennent lists several "practical implications" of the "challenge to approach the theological task from a more global perspective."[87] First, he says, the process of becoming "more informed and conversant with the growing theology from the Majority World church" might help broaden our horizons and heal our theological myopia.[88] Second, engagement with the theologies of the Majority World might help us by broadening our categories and challenging our systems of theology, especially when we are tempted to take these as finally definitive, or to think that they are the only important categories and questions. Third, and perhaps most importantly, "this open and honest exchange will help us recognize some of our own, less obvious, heresies and blind spots."[89]

I judge Tennent to be right; surely there are important opportunities for mutual enrichment. If analytic theologians will lift up their eyes to the fields, they will see that they are ripe for planting, cultivation and harvest. Genuine interreligious theological analysis is one such area where analytic theology can be especially important. Analytic theology may help us move beyond the fairly common types of social-scientific work that one often finds in interreligious studies to the kind of clear-eyed conceptual analysis and rigor of argument that is needed for progress. This work has begun in some ways; for instance, Harold Netland and Keith Yandell have done important work in Buddhist-Christian dialogue that is theologically rich and metaphysically serious.[90]

---

[85]Timothy C. Tennent, *Theology in the Context of World Christianity: How the Global Church Is Influencing the Way We Think About and Discuss Theology* (Grand Rapids: Zondervan, 2007), p. 2.
[86]Ibid.
[87]Ibid., p. 17.
[88]Tennent illustrates this myopia by reference to the 1991 publication of *Doing Theology in Today's World*, ed. John D. Woodbridge and Thomas E. McComiskey (Grand Rapids: Zondervan, 1991). Tennent notes that "the voices of Majority World theologians from Africa, India, China, and Korea are not heard," *Theology in the Context*, p. 17.
[89]Tennent, *Theology in the Context*, p. 18.
[90]Harold A. Netland and Keith E. Yandell, *Buddhism: A Christian Exploration and Appraisal* (Downers Grove, IL: IVP Academic, 2009).

Surely much work awaits. But beyond this sort of rigorous interreligious theological analysis, much work awaits on other theological topics as well.

To be sure, dealing with issues arising in global theology may seem strange (or worse) to many scholars in both the philosophical and theological guilds. To deal with such issues in a sustained and rigorous way—to take them seriously—might put the analytic theologian at risk of marginalization or ostracism. At this point we might usefully recall some important points from Alvin Plantinga's seminal "Advice to Christian Philosophers." Here he calls Christian philosophers (and, more generally, Christian intellectuals) to a more consistently and self-consciously Christian approach to their work. "First," he says,

> Christian philosophers and Christian intellectuals generally must display more autonomy—more independence from the rest of the philosophical world. Second, Christian philosophers must display more integrity—integrity in the sense of integral wholeness, or oneness, or unity, being all of one piece. . . . And necessary to these two is a third: Christian courage, or boldness, or strength, or perhaps Christian self-confidence. We Christian philosophers must display more faith, more trust in the Lord; we must put on the whole armor of God.[91]

Plantinga points out that the Christian in philosophy typically enters a top graduate program and is introduced to the "burning questions of the day" in the field: theories of reference;

> problems with probability; Quine's claims about the radical indeterminacy of translation; Rawls on justice; the causal theory of knowledge; Gettier problems; the artificial intelligence model for what it means to be a person; the question of the ontological status of unobservable entities in science; whether there is genuine objectivity in science or anywhere else; whether mathematics can be reduced to set theory . . . whether possible worlds are abstract or concrete,

and others.[92] He also recognizes that "the intellectual culture of our day is for the most part profoundly non-theistic and hence non-Christian—

---

[91]Alvin Plantinga, "Advice to Christian Philosophers," in *The Analytic Theist: An Alvin Plantinga Reader*, ed. James F. Sennett (Grand Rapids: Eerdmans, 1998), p. 297.
[92]Ibid., p. 298.

more than that, it is anti-theistic."[93] Thus such a student finds it "natural" to work on these topics "in the way she was taught to, thinking about them in light of the assumptions made by her mentors and in terms of currently accepted ideas as to what a philosopher should start from or take for granted, what requires argument and defense, and what a satisfying philosophical explanation or a proper resolution to a philosophical questions is like."[94] She will be "uneasy about departing widely from these topics and assumptions, feeling instinctively that any such departures are at best marginally respectable."[95]

Plantinga sees that from "one point of view" the common situation in philosophy is "natural and proper"—but from another "it is profoundly unsatisfactory."[96] The common issues and questions in mainstream philosophy and theology are indeed important, and Christians *should* be working on them. To think that we should not work on them, or to think that our nontheist and non-Christian colleagues have nothing to teach us, "would be a piece of foolish arrogance, belied by the fact of the matter."[97] To the contrary, "Christians have much to learn and much of enormous importance to learn by way of dialogue and discussion with their non-theistic colleagues," and they should be "intimately involved in the professional life of the philosophical community at large, both because of what they can learn and because of what they can contribute."[98] But such issues are not the only ones of importance, and such discussions are not the only ones that are legitimate. As Plantinga says, "The Christian community has its own questions, its own concerns, its own topics for investigation, its own agenda, its own research program."[99] Thus the Christian philosopher "may have to reject certain currently fashionable assumptions about the philosophic enterprise—he may have to reject widely accepted assumptions as to what are the proper starting points and procedures."[100] For Plantinga, "what is needed here is more

---

[93]Ibid., p. 297.
[94]Ibid., p. 298.
[95]Ibid.
[96]Ibid.
[97]Ibid., p. 314.
[98]Ibid.
[99]Ibid., p. 298.
[100]Ibid., p. 299.

independence, more autonomy with respect to the projects and concerns of the non-theistic philosophical world."[101]

I doubt that the general situation has changed all that much from Plantinga's original context in the 1980s (although the discussion has shifted significantly), and many people who approach the task of analytic theology with training in professional philosophy will recognize his description. It should not be at all surprising, then, that analytic theologians who hail from academic philosophy might not be prone to see work on some issues in global Christian theology as something that will be valued as interesting, important or respectable. In many ways, the situation is similar in mainstream academic theology. Plantinga is right that "a good bit of allegedly Christian theology is animated by a spirit wholly foreign to that of Christian theism"; but beyond this *geist* it is common for graduate students to be inducted into a fairly standard set of appropriate theological topics and methods for research.[102]

Plantinga's advice to Christian philosophers in general is relevant to analytic theologians in particular. Analytic theologians (especially those who hail from training in philosophy) need to be engaged with the ongoing conversations in mainstream philosophy; Christian analytic theologians who are trained in metaphysics, epistemology and ethics should be committed to those discussions. But this is not *all* they should do. Similarly, analytic theologians (especially those who come from training in theology) need to be engaged with work on more mainstream figures and issues in theology. But, again, this is not *all* they should do. As Plantinga says, we need more autonomy—and perhaps more imagination and more courage—in our work. For in addition to the questions and issues that animate mainstream discussions in philosophy and theology, Christians have their own issues and questions. Admittedly, in the case of some theological issues, some of these may seem strange and even bizarre. Fair enough. But they are also very important to many Christians—indeed, for some people these are, quite literally, matters of life and death.

We must also recognize that there are barriers to analytic engagement

---

[101]Ibid.
[102]Ibid., p. 298.

with these issues from the side of many "non-Westerners" as well. Analytic consideration of familiar and important issues in, say, religious epistemology or the metaphysics of divine action will seem as foreign to some non-Westerners as the issues themselves may seem to the analytic theologians. Some theologians will be tempted to respond as follows: "Epistemology? Epistemology is a Western concern. We don't need epistemology—we have stories."[103] Direct, focused and rigorous analysis of these issues with the use of the common analytic tools may strike some theologians as both naive and arrogant, and such analysis could elicit charges of "colonialism." Surely any analytic engagement (perhaps especially if undertaken by Europeans or Americans) will have to proceed with humility, openness and respect.

But while we need to recognize the obstacles and barriers, we also need to see that analytic theologians are equipped with some of the tools that might be important in such work. We need to be clear about the possibilities and potential of analytic theology here, and several caveats are important. First, analytic theologians do not have all the necessary tools, and to say that the issues are varied and complicated is to put it mildly. It is important not to have a hypertrophied sense of the importance or capabilities of analytic theology here (as elsewhere); it is not as if logical analysis of some key issues will suddenly "solve" all the problems. Neither, alas, will this resolve the critical human rights issues. Analytic theology is not the cure-all here, and we should not be tempted to think that merely expressing ourselves with more clarity and rigor (as in Michael Rea's P1-P5; see pp. 17-18) or offering metaphysical and epistemological analysis of the various claims made will somehow "fix" everything.

Second, I am *not* suggesting that a phalanx of "Western" analytic theologians needs to descend on, say, sub-Saharan Africa or southern India to sort out various theological conundrums for the pitiable "non-Westerners." Such an approach will likely only invite further criticisms of colonialism. Moreover, such a posture is deeply unhealthy for both Western theo-

---

[103]At a theological consultation on witchcraft accusations (held at Africa International University in Nairobi, Kenya [formerly Nairobi Evangelical Graduate School of Theology], in March 2012), I heard a Ghanaian theologian say this to a Nigerian theologian who raised some concerns and insisted that the epistemological issues must be faced squarely.

logian and indigenous theologian alike. It is unhealthy for the Westerners because it can tempt us to the arrogance and self-reliance to which we seem to be prone, and it is unhealthy as well because we may miss many important lessons and insights. And it is unhealthy for the non-Westerners because it may serve to deepen suspicions and thus block them from the reception of helpful resources. So this should not be a scenario where Western analytic theologians think that they are going to swoop in, fix a problem and then ride off into the sunset. Instead, any progress needs to be made in a truly collaborative way. What we need is more complex and messier: we need more Western theologians who have the humility and patience to learn from their global colleagues *and* more theologians from Africa, Asia and Oceania who are able to employ analytic skills and tools in a helpful way. In other words, we need both more autonomy from the nontheistic world and more actual integration (in a global sense). We do not need more colonialism, but we do need more truly global Christian theology. If this theology is truly global, it will not be—and cannot be—reducible to what "Westerners" say about "global" concerns. At the same time, however, if it is truly global, it will not remove or ignore insights and contributions from Europe, North America or Australasia. If it is truly *global* Christian theology, it *cannot* do so.

Finally, I do not mean to suggest that the only possible benefits in such engagement are unidirectional. (Even less do I mean to suggest that the one-way stream of benefits would go from "West" to "South.") It should be clear that I am convinced that analytic theology has helpful tools to offer in some of the issues arising in global Christian theology; beyond the kinds of general commitments to clarity and rigor that we see in Rea's P1-P5, the hard work done in religious epistemology and the metaphysics of divine and creaturely action might yield real benefits here. But perhaps the benefits may go the "other" way as well—maybe there are insights and lessons that the Western theologians need to learn too. At the very least, Western analytic theologians—including those who, like me, find themselves initially skeptical that there is anything supernatural afoot in, say, the vast majority of cases of purported witchcraft—should remain open to the possibility that "there are more things in heaven and earth, Horatio, than are dreamt of in your philosophy."[104]

In this section, I have suggested that analytic theology may be important in areas of inquiry—and geography—that to this point are underexplored and underdeveloped. I have suggested that the work of global analytic theology might be both beneficial and indeed urgent. Many areas of inquiry await in interreligious dialogue (done in an analytic key rather than in merely a social-science mode) and globalizing Christian theology. While it would be mistaken and probably dangerous for analytic theologians to think that their tools and skills are the only ones necessary, or even the most important, surely it would also be a shame for analytic theologians to ignore the places where they might be very helpful. What we need is "more courage, more thinking against the grain, more setting of one's own agenda, more mining of theology's own rich resources."[105]

---

[104]William Shakespeare, "The Tragedy of Hamlet, Prince of Denmark," act 1, scene 5, lines 166-67, in *The Riverside Shakespeare*, ed. G. Blakemore Evans (Boston: Houghton Mifflin, 1974), p. 1151.
[105]Wolterstorff, "To Theologians," p. 84.

Analytic Theology to the Glory of God

The criterion of past, future, and therefore present Christian utterance
is . . . Jesus Christ, God in His gracious revealing and reconciling address
to [humanity]. Does Christian utterance derive from Him?
Does it lead to Him? Is it conformable to Him?

KARL BARTH

THIS IS AN INVITATION TO ANALYTIC theology. I have suggested that theologians should be able and willing to do *analytic* theology. They should, in other words, do theology that is able and willing to employ the skills and tools of the analytic tradition. I have also urged analytic theologians to do *theology*. Analytic theology—*as theology*—should be (to borrow John Webster's phrase) "theological theology."[1] It should be grounded in Holy Scripture, informed by the Christian tradition and attentive to the potential and pressing challenges faced by God's people in God's world. But there is more—analytic theology should be oriented toward its proper end, and analytic theologians should be attentive to the proper approach and posture of theology.

Epigraph: Karl Barth, *Church Dogmatics*, I/1, *The Doctrine of the Word of God*, ed. T. F. Torrance, trans. Geoffrey Bromiley (Edinburgh: T & T Clark, 1975), p. 4.

[1] E.g., John Webster, *Confessing God: Essays in Christian Dogmatics* (New York: T & T Clark, 2005), pp. 11-32. See also Webster's insightful "What Makes Theology Theological?," *Journal of Analytic Theology* (2015): 17-28.

THE APPROACH OF THE THEOLOGIAN

For centuries, theologians have insisted that some particular qualities were important in the study of theology. Some of these are, of course, important in intellectual work generally, but they are especially important in divinity. As we might expect, these various lists of qualities include the acquisition of a body of knowledge and a professional skill set. But frequently the requirements of theology go far deeper—they move from intellectual ability and academic preparation to the "affections." As our theological forebears put it, such preparation includes "first, the attitude of the student and, second, the nontheological intellectual preparation of the student—in other words, preparation of the inward *habitus* and of the outward, objective, background knowledge."[2]

***Theology as* scientia.** Let us consider these elements of preparation in reverse order. Thomas C. Oden notes that from the earliest days of the study of theology as a discipline, Christians have recognized that the task "calls for many of the same intellectual abilities that are expected of the philosopher, logician, historian, and linguist," for the discipline requires "clear reasoning, right discernment of the relations between seemingly distant and varied teachings, multilayered powers of intuitive insight, sound movement from premises to conclusions, capacity for critical analysis, and the power of internally consistent reflection."[3] Concern for precision, clarity and argumentative rigor simply are part of the historic vision of what it means to do theology. And this concern is not limited to "scholastic" (as opposed to "pastoral," "practical" or "spiritual") theologians. As we have seen, even such pastoral theologians as the prominent evangelist John Wesley insist that logic is "necessary next to, and in order to, the knowledge of Scripture," for with it we have the possibility of "apprehending things clearly, judging truly, and reasoning conclusively."[4] Wesley also sees, by the way, that it is good "to make people talk less; by showing

---

[2]Richard A. Muller, *Post-Reformation Reformed Dogmatics: The Rise and Development of Reformed Orthodoxy, ca. 1520–ca. 1725*, vol. 1, *Prolegomena to Theology* (Grand Rapids: Baker Academic, 2003), p. 212.
[3]Thomas C. Oden, *The Living God: Systematic Theology* (San Francisco: HarperSanFrancisco, 1987), 1:359.
[4]John Wesley, "Address to the Clergy," in *The Works of John Wesley*, vol. 10, *Letters, Essays, Dialogs, and Addresses* (Grand Rapids: Zondervan, n.d.), p. 483.

them both what is, and what is not, to the point; and how extremely hard it is to prove anything."[5] He says similar things about the study of metaphysics. So the analytic ambitions of theology are nothing unusual in the Christian tradition, and the concerns that often animate contemporary work in analytic theology are not at all new or unique.

Historically, such concerns for precision, clarity and rigor were not isolated: the goal was to say something worthwhile, and to do so with precision, clarity and rigor *about something*. Argumentative rigor has its proper place, but logic serves to rightly order our thoughts rather than give us the proper content of those thoughts (in most theological cases). So for traditional ways of doing theology, the proper concern for precision, clarity and rigor can never displace proper attention to the sources and object of theology. Accordingly, while study of the arts and sciences is important for theology, knowledge of the central sources of theology is most vital.[6] Preeminent here is the study of Holy Scripture, and included is the study of the languages. John Wesley's series of questions to the clergy illustrates this:

> Have I, (1) such a knowledge of Scripture, as becomes him who undertakes so to explain it to others. . . . Upon the mention of any text, do I know the context, and the parallel place? . . . Do I know the scope of each book, and how every part tends thereto? Have I the skill to draw the natural inferences deducible from each text? (2) Do I understand Greek and Hebrew? Otherwise . . . am I not at the mercy of everyone who does understand, or pretends to understand, the original? For which way can I confute his pretense? Do I understand the language of the Old Testament? Critically? At all? Can I read into English one of David's Psalms; or even the first chapter of Genesis? Do I understand the language of the New Testament? Am I a critical master of it? Have I enough of it to read into English the first chapter of St. Luke?[7]

Wesley is not unique; to the contrary, he is representative of historic commitments to the theological task.

---

[5]Ibid., p. 492.

[6]Muller notes that the catalog of subjects that are "necessary" for the study of doctrine is "daunting": it includes "grammar, logic, and rhetoric (the *trivium*), arithmetic, geometry, music, and astronomy (the *quadrivium*), philosophy, physics, ethics, politics, oeconomics, metaphysics, history, architecture, and agriculture, and above all Latin, Greek, and Hebrew," *Prolegomena to Theology*, p. 210.

[7]Wesley, "Address to the Clergy," pp. 490-91.

In addition to the knowledge of Scripture, deep familiarity with the Christian tradition is also vitally important to the theological task. Again, Wesley's voice is representative when he asks: "Am I acquainted with the Fathers; at least those venerable men who lived in the earliest ages of the Church?"[8] "Who would not likewise desire to have some acquaintance with . . . St. Chrysostom, Basil, Jerome, [Augustine]; and, above all, the man of a broken heart, Ephraim Syrus?"[9]

How does all this have to do with the enterprise of contemporary analytic theology? A great deal, I think. For if analytic theology is to stand in continuity with theology as traditionally conceived, it will seek to be informed by the resources of the Christian tradition as well as engaged with the specialized study of those resources. If analytic theology is to be theology done in service to the people of God and for the sake of the world, it will do no less. And if analytic theology is to be theology that is done *coram Deo* and in obedience to God's gracious revelation, it cannot do less.

This means that the task of the analytic theologian has gotten harder rather than easier. In fact, it may look unrealistic, and to pretend otherwise may be misleading. William J. Abraham, a defender and practitioner of it, considers the following objection to analytic theology:

> Analytic theology appears totally unrealistic when you look at what is needed to get the job done in theology. Theology is an all-encompassing field. It involves initiation into several ancient and modern languages, into the historical study of scripture, into the history of the church and its teachings, and into normative assessment of the practices, ethics, and doctrines of the tradition; it also involves forays into other disciplines like sociology, philosophy, and the like. Imagine a theologian showing up and offering to do philosophy without serious immersion in the whole history of philosophy (ancient, medieval, and modern), and without first-order work in epistemology, normative ethics, metaphysics, logic, and philosophy of language. The whole idea of analytic theology looks hopelessly unrealistic, if you add up the dispositions and skills that have to be attained.[10]

---

[8]Ibid., p. 492.

[9]Ibid., p. 484.

[10]William J. Abraham, "Turning Philosophical Water into Theological Wine," *Journal of Analytic Theology* (2013): 4.

Abraham points out that "even theologians fail again and again" at the task of systematic theology.[11] I judge Abraham to be largely correct in his assessment that theologians fail at this task, and I think he is right to observe that much of what passes for "systematic" or "dogmatic" theology is really better understood as work in the history of modern theology. And I agree with him that the task seems daunting. For analytic theologians trained in theology, gaining facility with the important philosophical tools looks daunting indeed. For analytic theologians who are primarily trained in philosophy, however, gaining the requisite knowledge base (of the Christian Bible, of the tradition of patristic, medieval, Reformation/early modern, modern, and contemporary theology, and of important pastoral and cultural issues) to do analytic theology well is also a stiff challenge.

Recognizing that "theologians routinely draw upon a wide range of disciplines and apply them to a complex set of loci," Marc Cortez underscores the nature of this challenge.[12] Warning us not to "kid ourselves into thinking that even professional theologians have acquired any significant mastery of the many areas and disciplines involved," Cortez notes that we all tend to specialize in different areas and then rely on the work of other specialists where needed.[13] But this is, he rightly points out, a "problem with the nature of academic specialization as it is practiced in the academy today."[14] Cortez argues that "given the disciplinary breadth of theology, such academic ghettoization needs to stop."[15] Cortez is right. The answer is not to make every theologian a complete generalist who has no area of specialization. But neither is the current tendency toward intellectual Balkanization either helpful or sustainable in theology. A much more realistic—and, I think, much healthier—alternative is this: the analytic theologian should gain at least the minimal skills and knowledge that are necessary to engage with the various relevant disciplines, learning from them as well as speaking into them with

---

[11]Ibid.
[12]Marc Cortez, "As Much as Possible: Essentially Contested Concepts and Analytic Theology; A Response to William J. Abraham," *Journal of Analytic Theology* (2013): 22.
[13]Ibid.
[14]Ibid.
[15]Ibid.

competency (and, sometimes, from an importantly different perspective). Using this knowledge and these skills to engage the relevant disciplinary specializations, and learning from them, she then can reply on them with appropriate confidence.

Theology as scientia and sapientia. In addition to outward, objective preparation, the theological task also requires cultivation of "the inward *habitus*" of the theologian. The Protestant scholastics held that personal piety is "primary among the character traits of the theological student," and this is "essentially a fear of God (*timor Dei*)," which is, "as Scripture teaches, the primary ground (*principium*) of both true knowledge and wisdom (*scientia et sapientia*)."[16] On Richard Muller's summary, "Qualities of teachableness (*docilitas*) and zeal (*sedulitas*) or diligence (*diligentia*) manifest, at least in part, through the absence of perverse love, hate, anger, pride, and despair."[17] Similarly, Thomas Oden summarizes Thomas Aquinas's stipulations: the work of theology depends "through grace upon certain intellectual and moral virtues for its proper accomplishment: patience, love of truth, courage to follow one's convictions, humility in the face of the facts, loyalty to the truth, and a profound sense of awe in the presence of the truth."[18]

Drawing from the depth and breadth of the theological tradition, Oden identifies several "dispositions" or "habits of mind" that are important in the theological task. While agreeing with Oden that sometimes "modern skepticism may disparage these qualities," I think these are very important for analytic theologians to consider as they move forward in their work. Oden first highlights the need for "humility in the face of truth."[19] He recognizes that "the very greatness of the subject matter can tend to intoxicate," and "those who come under its influence may wrongly imagine that they are thereby morally above other Christians."[20] Surely Oden is right that this a danger, and I would add that another and closely related danger is also present: the temptation to imagine that they are intellectually superior to other Christians. The

---

[16]Muller, *Prolegomena to Theology*, p. 212.
[17]Ibid.
[18]Oden, *Living God*, 1:360.
[19]Ibid., 1:355.
[20]Ibid., 1:363.

study of theology may, in fallen creatures, elicit pride and a sense of moral superiority. But it may also give the theologian an inflated sense of intellectual superiority. When analytic theologians think they are "the intellectual ninjas of theology" (as I once heard a very bright young scholar say at a conference in analytic theology), surely the temptation to vanity and smugness is present. And while this temptation is in no way limited to the domains of analytic theologians, perhaps the concerns for high standards of rigor and argument are particularly fertile ground for such temptations. Like other sinners, analytic theologians need to be admonished by James: "God opposes the proud but shows favor to the humble" (Jas 4:6). Perhaps analytic theology is more prone to the vice of pride. Maybe it is, maybe it isn't; surely that doesn't matter all that much. What does seem to be true is this: the temptation to this vice is real. So let the analytic theologian humble himself till he is like this child, and then he will be the greatest in the kingdom of heaven (Mt 18:4).

Closely connected to humility is the importance of reverence and awe.[21] Surely "the fear of the LORD is the beginning of knowledge" (Prov 1:7), and there is no reason to think that the analytic theologian might be exempt from this dictum. Always and everywhere in Scripture we see that genuine encounter with God—and thus genuine knowledge of God—produces a response that is marked by a deep sense of human inadequacy. Given our finitude and our fallenness, how could it be otherwise? If Christian teaching about God is even generally correct, how can finite human creatures have genuine knowledge of God as their Creator and not shake their heads in wonder? And if we are, as Christian doctrine teaches us, sinners who have twisted and perverted ourselves, how can we not be completely awed by knowledge of God as our Redeemer? On the other hand, when God-talk becomes an occasion for our own aggrandizement and gives us an inflated sense of self-importance, rather than an occasion that produces genuine reverence and a deep sense of awe, something has gone badly awry.

Oden mentions patience as well, which he describes as "the habitual disposition to bear with trials and frustrations without complaint, to

---

[21]Oden's treatment is in ibid., 1:355-56.

exercise forbearance under difficulties, to be undisturbed by obstacles, delays, and failures, and to persevere with diligence until an issue is further resolved or rightly grasped."[22] Surely analytic theologians would do well to hear and heed this counsel, but it may be that the analytic traits can actually be helpful in the cultivation of patience as an important intellectual virtue. For steady, hard, careful and rigorous analytic work is rarely quick or easy, and often it requires diligent and steadfast endurance. As we have seen Wesley say, careful analysis shows "how hard it is to prove anything."[23]

Oden argues that theological work also involves a crucial element that is easily overlooked or forgotten. This element, he says, is "prayer for divine illumination and instruction."[24] Genuine theology, he insists, involves the cultivation of prayer as a habit and an attitude of prayer as an affection. Theology begins, he says, with "an attitude of openness and receptivity to God, inviting God's presence and inspiration to enable one's thoughts to be, so far as possible, fitting to the divine reality."[25] Genuine theology thus follows the supplication of the psalmist:

Open my eyes that I may see
    wonderful things in your law.

I am a stranger on earth;
    do not hide your commands from me. (Ps 119:18-19)

And it follows the admonition of James: "If any of you lacks wisdom, you should ask God, who gives generously to all without finding fault, and it will be given to you" (Jas 1:5). Lack of prayer, on the other hand, tends to foster both discouragement and pride. After all, as Dietrich Bonhoeffer reminds us, the setting of the first temptation and the primal sin is during the first theological conversation; it is in the "first conversation *about* God, the first religious, theological conversation."[26] Prayer reminds us of our place in the process of theology; we only and always receive

---

[22]Ibid., 1:356.
[23]Wesley, "Address to the Clergy," p. 492.
[24]Oden, *Living God*, 1:356.
[25]Ibid.
[26]Dietrich Bonhoeffer, *Creation and Fall, Temptation: Two Biblical Studies* (New York: Simon & Schuster, 1997), p. 76.

knowledge of the things of God as a gift, and we can never presume on it. Accordingly, we should receive it with humility and gratitude.

Oden observes that "if the study of God remains unaccompanied by 'the obedience of faith' (Rom 1:26), it is likely to become undisciplined self-expression." Thus "no temperament is more important to responsible theology than obedience, or radical responsiveness, to the divine address. . . . Obedience implies not merely hearing the truth, but acting upon it so as to embody it in one's life."[27] The concern for integrity is closely related. Thus "Jesus distinguished teaching out of one's own egocentricity from teaching God's truth: 'Anyone whose teaching is merely his own, aims at honour for himself. But if a man aims at the honour of him who sent him he is sincere, and there is nothing false in him' (John 7:17-18)."[28]

Finally, Oden mentions the importance of "willingness to suffer for the truth." As he sees it, "No Christian teacher or exponent is worth listening to who is not willing to suffer if need be for the truth of what is taught."[29] As he puts it, "Jesus did not hesitate to make it clear that his disciples must be prepared to 'be handed over for punishment and execution; and men of all nations will hate you for your allegiance to me' (Matt 24:9)."[30] Oden points out that Luther considered "prayer, meditation, and affliction (*oratio, meditatio, tentatio*)" as vital in the study of theology:

> This is the touchstone, this teaches you not merely to know and understand, but also to experience how right, how true, how sweet, how lovely, how mighty, how consoling, God's Word is, wisdom above all wisdom . . . through the raging of the devil they have so buffeted, distressed, and terrified me that they have made me a fairly good theologian, which I would not have become without them.[31]

Theology is not—and cannot be—a merely intellectual exercise if it involves genuine knowledge of God. Accordingly, analytic theology is

---

[27]Oden, *Living God*, 1:356-57.
[28]Ibid., 1:357.
[29]Ibid., 1:358.
[30]Ibid.
[31]Ibid., 1:358-59.

not—and cannot be—a merely intellectual exercise if it involves genuine knowledge of God.

THE TELOS OF THEOLOGY

What is theology ultimately about? What—and *who*—is it really for? I suggest that we think about analytic theology this way: *as theology*, analytic theology should strive to speak truthfully of God in a manner that glorifies him, and in doing so it should serve to edify God's people. Thomas Aquinas puts it this way: "The chief aim of sacred doctrine is to teach the knowledge of God, not only as he is in himself, but also as he is the beginning of things and their last end."[32] The Reformed scholastic Francis Turretin modifies this theme only slightly: "All things are discussed in theology either because they deal with God himself or have a relation to him as the first principle and ultimate end."[33] William J. Abraham's summary echoes this conviction in many respects: "The theologian's responsibility is to speak of God and of everything else insofar as it relates to God."[34] And if analytic theology really is "systematic theology attuned to the skills, resources, and virtues of analytic philosophy," then the task of the analytic theologian is also "to speak of God and of everything else insofar as it relates to God."[35]

I have tried to make a case that the task of the analytic theologian is broader than we sometimes tend to think. It is also, however, very pointed and particular. For the task of the theologian is not merely to say things about God (or God-and-everything)—it is to speak *truly* of God (so far as we can) and to do so in a way that celebrates the glory of God's being and actions. As Turretin puts it, God is "not to be regarded simply as God in himself . . . but as he is our God (i.e., covenanted in Christ as he has revealed himself to us in his word not only as the object of knowledge, but also of worship. True religion (which

---

[32]Thomas Aquinas, *Summa Theologica* I.2, trans. the Fathers of the Dominican Province (New York: Benzinger Brothers, 1948).

[33]Francis Turretin, *Institutes of Elenctic Theology*, trans. George Musgrave Giger, ed. James Dennison Jr. (Phillipsburg, NJ: P & R, 1992), p. 16.

[34]William J. Abraham, "Turning Philosophical Water into Theological Wine," *Journal of Analytic Theology* (2013): 4.

[35]Ibid., p. 5.

theology teaches) consists of these two things."[36]

So if we do analytic theology but do not do our best to speak truthfully of God, then we simply have not done our job. Theology done as mere "bull session" is ultimately pointless—and it likely leads to idolatry.[37] If that is all we can do, then we have failed at our calling. Our calling is to speak truthfully of God.

And if we do analytic theology in a way that promotes ourselves rather than glorify God, then we have not done our job. We have failed; indeed, we have failed miserably. This is not to say that all projects in analytic theology should begin with a prayer meeting and conclude with an altar call. Neither is it to suggest that all analytic theology be "popular" in level, or that it must be reducible to "devotional" reading. Not at all; we need to pursue analytic theology with all the rigor we can muster.

Finally, analytic theology—*as theology*—should serve the church and the world. None of what I say here is to decry or belittle the vitally important *critical* function of analytic theology. Sometimes brush needs to be cleared, and the tools of analytic theology often serve admirably in that task. But in both its critical and constructive modes, analytic theology can serve God and God's purposes in the world. And—as theology—it should do so.

AN INVITATION TO ANALYTIC THEOLOGY, AND SOME MODEST SUGGESTIONS

Analytic theology, conceived of as "systematic theology attuned to the skills, resources, and virtues of analytic philosophy" (so Abraham, and valuing Rea's P1-P5, see chap. 1), has much to offer constructive Christian theology as it moves forward. Theologians can benefit from the "skills" and "resources" of the analytic tradition, and engagement with it might yield more clarity and rigor in the discipline. At the same time, philosophers of religion who are interested in theological issues might benefit from more direct engagement with the sources and methods of theology.

---

[36]Turretin, *Institutes*, p. 16.

[37]See Randal Rauser, "Theology as Bull Session," in *Analytic Theology: New Essays in the Philosophy of Theology*, ed. Oliver D. Crisp and Michael C. Rea (Oxford: Oxford University Press, 2009), pp. 70-84.

As I see things, this is the time for us to step out of our disciplinary for-
tresses, repent (where we must) of our arrogance and defensiveness and
pursue genuinely interdisciplinary work. I make the following suggestions in hopes of genuine progress.

Analytic and modern theology. Analytic theologians would do well
to engage directly and charitably with the major figures and movements
in modern and contemporary theology. Some analytic philosophers of
religion may think there is little to be gained from such an exercise; it
seems to some of them as though modern and contemporary theology
is just too confused and too confusing to be worth the effort. On this
understanding, modern theology lost its way when it traded in its birthright for a mess of Continental porridge and postmodern poison. Accordingly, there is nothing to be gained from careful engagement with
modern theology and theologians; for anything worthwhile can be found
elsewhere, and if you look for what is worthwhile elsewhere, you won't
have to wade through so much misguided nonsense and incoherent
garbage. This is, it seems, sometimes the temptation that besets the proponent of analytic theology.

But while I understand this temptation (and confess that sometimes
I have sympathy for it), I am convinced that such a dismissive attitude
would be misguided and unfortunate. Analytic theology needs, I think,
to engage with modern and contemporary theology for several reasons.
First, charitable engagement is needed for pragmatic reasons. Theologians are not all that likely to be enchanted by the notion that "philosophers" with much less technical training in the sources and methods of
theology are really that much better equipped than they are to understand their subject matter. Any approach that smacks of the notion that
"we don't have your training in the various subfields of theology, but we
really don't even need it, because we are smarter than you and now we're
thinking really hard about the issues that you've stumbled around for so
long" is very likely to alienate professional theologians. And I am confident that such alienation is not good for the future of analytic theology.
The success of the endeavor depends on genuinely interdisciplinary work,
and this in turn depends, in large part, on mutual goodwill. This is not
the time for intellectual snobbery—in either direction. So if analytic

theologians want to gain a hearing within more mainstream systematic or constructive theology, it will need to show respect and charity; it will need to take the work of the theologians seriously.[38]

Second, charitable engagement is important because there simply is no going around the problems, challenges and opportunities of the modern era. Analytic theologians may (or, of course, may not) think that the major responses of many modern theologians to the challenges of modernity were misguided and flawed. They may think that the prominent theologians of the modern era chose poorly in terms of philosophical mentors and conversation partners. They may judge the resultant product to be deeply flawed and misguided. They may think that it is of dubious coherence, and they may shake their heads at the elements of the classical tradition that the modern theologians so quickly surrendered or jettisoned. They may also, of course, shake their heads in bewilderment at what the modern theologians held on to; they may wonder, "Why were they so stubborn about *that*?" Even so, however—and even where the analytic theologian judges the work of the modern theologians to be deficient—it may be that the struggles of the modern era are instructive, and constructive analytic theology might benefit from seeing such struggles within their intellectual and social contexts.

Finally, perhaps the analytic theologian actually has something to learn (in a positive sense) from modern and contemporary theology. Contemporary theologians tend to be very well aware of how theology is interwoven with a wide range of social, ethical and political concerns. They are often keenly aware of such issues, and they are exercised to bring theology to bear on them. Perhaps this is one way—among many others—that analytic theologians might actually benefit from engagement with modern and contemporary theology. In other words, analytic theologians might find that their horizons are broadened by learning from modern theology as they are pushed further into engagement with the natural and social sciences as well as cultural and ethical concerns. In addition, of course, they should be open to the possibility that their understandings might be deepened by such engagement.

---

[38]A stellar example of such work is Kevin Diller, "Is God *Necessarily* Who God Is? Alternatives for the Trinity and Election Debate," *Scottish Journal of Theology* (2013): 209-20.

To assume anything less, it seems to me, is simply hubris.

Analytic theology and the theological interpretation of Scripture.
Analytic theology, if it really is to be theology, should be rooted and
grounded in divine revelation. Accordingly, the revelation of God in the
incarnation of the Son must be decisive. And for Christian theologians
who think God has revealed himself in or through Scripture, engagement
with Scripture is of vital importance. Let me first say what this claim
doesn't mean. First, I do not mean to suggest that the analytic theologian
has nothing to contribute to theology unless she is also an expert in the
Hebrew Bible/Christian Old Testament and in New Testament studies.
The study required for genuine expertise in biblical studies is vast, and
the requisite skills and background knowledge (including study of the
biblical languages as well as cognate and neighboring languages, ancient
Near Eastern, Greco-Roman or Mediterranean, and Second Temple
Jewish historical and cultural backgrounds, historical-critical methods
and conclusions, the history of interpretation, literary criticism, and of
course the exegesis of particular texts and their place within various
corpora and the canon) take a veritable lifetime to master. To suggest
that the analytic theologian must have genuine expertise in all these
fields is unrealistic and likely pretentious. Membership in the guild of
biblical studies should not be a prerequisite for analytic theologians.
Second, I do not mean to suggest that every treatise in analytic theology
should be reduced to an exercise in biblical exegesis, or even that all work
in analytic theology should begin with biblical exegesis.

Nonetheless, engagement with Scripture is of vital importance for
Christian theologians. I've indicated a bit of what I don't mean when I
say this, so let me also say what I do take this claim to mean. First, analytic theologians should know Scripture itself well enough that they are
able to relate their work to what the Bible may have to say about the topic
or issue under discussion, and to know if the clear implications of scriptural affirmations impinge on it either directly or indirectly. Recall Karl
Barth's admonition: "Exegesis, exegesis, exegesis."[39] Second, they should
know enough about the scholarly study of the Bible that they are able to

---

[39]Karl Barth, in Eberhard Busch, *Karl Barth: His Life from Letters and Autobiographical Texts*
(Philadelphia: Fortress, 1976), p. 259.

engage with it and benefit from it. Third, they should know enough about such scholarly work in biblical studies to offer their own questions and criticisms when these are appropriate.[40] Finally, they should realize that analytic theology might best be done within a community of scholars where there is appropriate division of labor, cross-fertilization, mutually beneficial correction and feedback. Throughout their work, analytic theologians must be engaged with the *Sache* of Scripture—and thus they must work with the actual text of Scripture.[41]

In particular, work at the intersection of analytic theology and the "theological interpretation of Scripture" holds great promise. As Daniel J. Treier describes it, theological interpretation of Scripture holds much in common with traditional Christian readings of the Bible: "Christians read the Bible as Scripture, authoritative as God's Word for faith and life; thus, to interpret Scripture was to encounter God."[42] And while it is not (or need not be) opposed to historical-critical studies, it is not always either committed to those methods or accountable to the conclusions reached by such studies. It tends to view the Christian tradition as an aid and ally in the interpretation of the Bible; often it values "precritical" exegesis. It has space for various forms of "postcolonial" as well as "post-critical" interpretation, and often its practitioners place a high premium on "canonical theology." Consistently, "theological exegesis deals with the Bible as a word about God and from God."[43]

This movement is burgeoning. It exhibits much variety, and it holds great promise. It is, I think, a very natural conversation partner for ana-

---

[40]E.g., C. Stephen Evans, *The Historical Christ and the Jesus of Faith: The Incarnational Narrative as History* (Oxford: Oxford University Press, 1996); Alvin Plantinga, *Warranted Christian Belief* (Oxford: Oxford University Press, 2000), pp. 374-421; William P. Alston, "Historical Criticism of the Synoptic Gospels," in *"Behind" the Text: History and Biblical Interpretation*, ed. Craig Bartholomew, C. Stephen Evans, Mary Healy and Murray Rae (Grand Rapids: Zondervan, 2003), pp. 151-80; Peter van Inwagen, "Critical Studies of the New Testament and the User of the New Testament," in *Hermes and Athena: Biblical Exegesis and Philosophical Theology*, ed. Thomas P. Flint and Eleonore Stump (Notre Dame, IN: University of Notre Dame Press, 1993), pp. 159-90. See also the pushback from C. L. Brinks, "On Nail Scissors and Toothbrushes: Responding to the Philosophers' Critiques of Historical Biblical Criticism," *Religious Studies* (2013): 357-76.

[41]See Webster's incisive comments on the importance of a comprehensive approach, "What Makes Theology Theological," pp. 27-28.

[42]Daniel J. Treier, *Introducing Theological Interpretation of Scripture: Recovering a Christian Practice* (Grand Rapids: Baker Academic, 2008), p. 13.

[43]Ibid., p. 36.

lytic theology. And it will be, I hope, the next frontier for analytic theology.

Analytic theology and Christian tradition. Similarly, analytic theology will flourish as theology, and best serve the church, as it commits to serious engagement with the resources and insights of the Christian tradition. Contemporary analytic theologians may sometimes—perhaps often—judge the tradition to have erred in important ways. They may conclude that sometimes the theologians of the patristic, medieval and early modern eras took the wrong turn, or in other cases they followed the right course but simply did not go far enough. In these cases, contemporary analytic theologians may learn from the mistakes and missteps of their forebears. In other instances, theologians doing constructive analytic work can benefit from the great work done by their forefathers and foremothers. Either way (and I must confess that I generally find much more to appreciate than to denigrate), contemporary analytic theology stands to benefit. Simply put, analytic theology needs more careful and well-informed work in "retrieval theology."

Analytic theology and global Christian theology. I have pointed out that the burgeoning movements associated with "global Christian theology" offer opportunities for engagement and growth. Analytic theology may be better for engagement with theological issues in the Majority World (or Global South or Two-Thirds World). And analytic theology may be able to provide some of the skills and resources that would be helpful to the theologies that are developing in various contexts where a wide range of issues may be faced. What is needed is a broader awareness of, and sensitivity to, as well as the commitment and ability to humbly engage with, this wide and ever-widening range of theological issues and challenges. Such engagement is fraught with perils from various sides, and it almost certainly will not be easy. But it is too important to ignore.

Analytic theology and the care of souls. It seems plain to me that analytic theology should also be attuned to its relation to the care of souls. Some analytic theologians may resist this connection; some may remonstrate that the work of conceptual analysis is far removed from the spiritual life of Christian pilgrims. But if analytic theology really is theology—if it intends to speak as truthfully as possible about God and everything else as it is related to God—then it must face up to its pastoral responsibility.

To be clear, I do not mean by this to suggest that the work of analytic theologians must always be aimed at "popular" audiences (or even directed at working pastors and priests). Surely this can be a blessing when done well, and just as surely there is room for a great deal more analytic "public theology" that is done well.[44] But I am not suggesting that analytic theology should always be done in this mode or pitched at this level; neither do I mean to suggest that it should be "dumbed down." Instead, I am talking more generally about the need for analytic theologians to approach their task with appropriate sensitivity to the depth of affective issues in theology. Consider the case studies I have employed to this point. In very different ways, all of them have serious pastoral consequences, and in each case analytic theology that is done well can be pastorally helpful. Taking them in reverse order, one does not have to look far to see how issues related to the intersection of faith and science are potentially troublesome for many Christians. Many people (on both sides of the issues) claim that the only legitimate options are "evolution" or "creation"; and sometimes Christians are told that one must either believe that the earth is no more than a few thousand years old or deny their faith and their Savior. In such situations, theological work that is both careful and informed can be pastorally helpful, and the analytic tradition can bring tools and skills that are appropriate and helpful in this work. When we turn to the metaphysics of the incarnation, at first glance it may seem that these issues are further removed from Christian discipleship and the care of souls. But first glances can be deceiving. As a pastor of congregations in southwestern Michigan and south-central Alaska, I have known many people who believed—sometimes very deeply and even fiercely—that the truly human Jesus was also somehow fully divine and one with his Father, that his life, death and resurrection were somehow deeply meaningful because of who he was, and that

---

[44]Sterling examples of this are not hard to find; just on the problem of evil, see, e.g., Michael C. Rea, "Divine Hiddenness, Divine Silence," in *Philosophy of Religion: An Anthology*, ed. Louis Pojman and Michael C. Rea, 6th ed. (Boston: Wadsworth, 2012), pp. 266-75; Eleonore Stump, *Wandering in Darkness: Narrative and the Problem of Suffering* (Oxford: Oxford University Press, 2010); Alvin Plantinga, *God, Freedom, and Evil* (Grand Rapids: Eerdmans, 1974).

somehow his Spirit was with them in the midst of their deepest sorrows and highest joys. They found great meaning and comfort in this belief, but sometimes they were also aware of challenges to the doctrine. So while the mode of discourse that is common in analytic theology would have been unfamiliar to them, the basic issues were not.[45] Similarly, many Christians are deeply interested in issues relating to divine providence and sovereignty, on one hand, and human responsibility and freedom, on the other hand. Even though issues at the intersection of Scripture and metaphysics can be complicated, the basic and underlying issues are of interest to many Christians.

CONCLUSION

Theology needs the resources of the analytic tradition. As Fred Sanders observes, "The kind of systematic theology that is heavily informed by biblical exegesis and the history of doctrine would benefit greatly from the conceptual clarity which could be provided by the kind of philosophical theology that concentrates on analytic tasks."[46] But analytic theology also needs to be *theology*; it needs to be grounded in Scripture, informed by the Christian tradition and alert to its ecclesial and cultural contexts. As Sanders says, "Philosophical theology could benefit from a closer encounter with the great themes of the Christian heritage, and a better understanding of the Biblical logic by which those themes emerged into conceptual form."[47]

Analytic theology is an energetic and promising development in Christian theology. Whether it is best understood as a new movement or as a vibrant renewal of older ways of doing theology, it seems to have a bright future. The time is ripe, then, for analytic theologians to "step forward with humble boldness, intellectual imagination, and spiritual seriousness, drawing from the wells of Scripture and the deep resources

---

[45]This point echoes one made in Thomas McCall, "Theologians, Philosophers, and the Doctrine of the Trinity," in *Philosophical and Theological Essays on the Trinity*, ed. Thomas McCall and Michael C. Rea (Oxford: Oxford University Press, 2009), p. 348.
[46]Fred Sanders, "The State of the Doctrine of the Trinity in Evangelical Theology," *Southwestern Journal of Theology* (2005): 170.
[47]Ibid.

of two millennia of Christian theology."[48] Perhaps, by God's grace, it can be used by God for the broad and deep spiritual purposes of theology. Perhaps, by God's grace, it can speak rightly of the triune God of holy love. And perhaps, by God's grace, it will result in love of God and neighbor.

---

[48]Nicholas Wolterstorff, "To Theologians: From One Who Cares About Theology but Is Not One of You," *Theological Education* (2005): 85.

Author Index

Subject Index

Finding the Textbook You Need

The IVP Academic Textbook Selector
is an online tool for instantly finding the IVP books
suitable for over 250 courses across 24 disciplines.

---

ivpacademic.com